All Best Wishes

& Love

Kevin Lloyd

'Tosh'

THE MAN WHO LOVED TOO MUCH

KEVIN LLOYD

WITH

STAFFORD HILDRED

BLAKE

Published by Blake Publishing Ltd,
3 Bramber Court, 2 Bramber Road, London W14 9PB,
England

First published in Great Britain 1997

ISBN 1 85782 191 2

British Library Cataloguing-in-Publication Data:
A catalogue record for this book is available
from the British Library.

Typeset by BCP

Printed in Great Britain by Creative Print and Design (Wales),
Ebbw Vale, Gwent

1 3 5 7 9 10 8 6 4 2

Pictures reproduced by kind permission of
the author, EMI, Granada TV, *Derby Evening Telegraph*,
Chris Rushton, Bill Cooper, *Daily Express*,
Solo Syndication, Pearson TV.

Every effort has been made to contact the relevant copyright-holders, but some were
unobtainable. We would be grateful if the appropriate owners would contact us.

To my children:
Mark, Sophie, Chloe, James,
Poppy, Henry, Edward and Elly.

And to Rita,
who has helped me to live again.

CONTENTS

INTRODUCTION

Sometimes I have to pinch myself to make sure that it is all really happening to me. It's only a couple of years ago that I used to have the dream marriage. I was still deeply in love with Lesley, the woman I moved in with only a few weeks after we met back in 1975. And I thought she felt the same way. We had a wonderful lifestyle — seven fantastic children, a lovely house in the country, and I had a rewarding job on one of Britain's most popular television series.

Well, I've still got the job. But somehow the dream has turned into a nightmare and my secure and happy life has been taken away from me. Lesley and I have parted on the most publicly acrimonious terms imaginable. I am living in a small rented flat and my children haven't spoken to me for more than a year.

Unless you've been holidaying on Mars for a couple of years, you'll have heard Lesley's colourful views on our split. Underneath huge headlines and on receipt of large cheques, she has gone into great detail in long and, for me, excruciatingly painful, articles about the break-up of our marriage. I thought I was a good husband and I was certainly always faithful, but I've been branded a 'boozing womaniser' who would turn into a brutal monster every time he touched a drop of alcohol.

I've been ordered out of our house, instructed to find treatment for my drinking, I've become estranged from my children and publicly humiliated at every turn. Lesley has told every journalist who will listen that I am the next step down from the Devil incarnate. She has staged a one-woman campaign with a placard outside the studios of *The Bill* demanding more money from me. She has talked her way into television studios to criticise me. She even lobbied the MPs at Westminster about her situation.

Lesley now clearly hates me with exactly the same sort of overwhelming passion that made our happy years together so fantastic. The last time we met, at yet another agonising divorce court hearing, I quietly asked her if she would give the children my love and her face twisted with anger as she snapped, 'No'. And, presumably, in case I was still in any doubt about her feelings for me, she whispered 'Bastard'. Perhaps wisely, the judge chose not to hear.

And one of the worst things is that I still don't understand how it has come to this. I don't hate Lesley. In fact, somewhere very deep down inside, I still love her. How can you spend 20 happy years and have seven wonderful children with someone and not still feel some sort of love? She was a marvellous wife to me and a wonderful mother to our children. The tabloids have offered me a fortune to get my own back and slate her in public, but I'm just not interested in any kind of revenge.

I am writing this book for my children. For Mark and for Sophie and for Chloe and for James and for Poppy and for Henry and for Edward and for Elly. I want them to know my side of the story, but I don't want it just twisted and edited and splashed underneath some sensational headline. I want to tell it in my way in this book. And I want the chance to tell them that, whatever happens, I will always love them all. I am desperately sad about what has happened between Lesley and me and, although most of what she has said in the Press is either horribly distorted or simply untrue, I do admit that most of the blame for our initial split was mine.

But I want to tell the whole of my story, and it hasn't all been bitterness and tears by any means.

CHAPTER ONE

CHILDHOOD

I was born in The City Hospital, Derby, on 28 March 1949, and my first home was a police house, 54 Radford Street in Alvaston, a suburb of Derby. My father was the local copper and we lived on an estate. There were two police houses, and at that time my dad was a Constable in the Derby Borough force. After that he became a Detective Constable, rather like DC Tosh Lines in *The Bill*. It was when he was a detective that he made most of his friends, but the hours were so long that my mum finally objected to never seeing him. He went back into uniform and finished up as Station Sergeant in charge of Peartree Police Station in Derby.

My dad's name was Ellis Aled Lloyd, and he came from a little village called Yspytty-y-fan, (Welsh for St

John's Hospital), near Betws-y-Coed in Snowdonia, North Wales, and he was very Welsh indeed. He served in the RAF in the War. When he joined up he couldn't speak a word of English, but he soon learned. His father died early and he was brought up by his mum. He ran away to try to join the Army when he was only 14, but was brought back and had to wait his turn.

Dad became an engineer in the RAF and was shot in Belgium towards the end of the War. He spent quite a time in hospital there having treatment after being hit by shrapnel. Some of it went into his eye but, luckily, he made an almost complete recovery, although he did have trouble with his eye for the rest of his life.

After the War, he moved to Derby because his sister, Katherine, was living here. There was no work in Wales. He lived in Derby and he first met my mother, Agnes Amelia Brennan as she then was, in the Blue Peter pub in Alvaston. He was having a drink and my mother just happened to be in there with her mother and stepfather. He said later that he was immediately attracted to her and, being a traditional sort of gentleman, he courteously went up and asked my grandmother in his strong Welsh accent if he could ask my mother out.

She was surprised by the polite request from the odd-sounding stranger, but she gave her permission and their first date was at the Broadway Hotel in Derby. My dad had left the RAF to become a fireman on the railway by then. For a very brief time in between he had been a professional boxer. He had only had about five fights when he was knocked out in the first round on Blackpool Pier. It was such a flooring he came round and said to himself, 'This is a stupid way of earning a living.' He was a good boxer. He had been RAF champion, but when he turned pro he found himself in a different league altogether.

They got married in 1948 and I came along in 1949. It was a very happy home. We weren't well off but I never wanted for anything. My earliest memories are of trips to the seaside and lots of laughter. My father was three years younger than my mother and I remember she made him grow a moustache because he looked too young. That's not why I've got one, because I definitely look old enough without it. He was always in plain clothes, so the first time he came home in his police uniform, I didn't recognise him.

We were the police family on the estate and times were very different then. Sometimes, people who weren't too enthusiastic about the forces of law and order used to call us 'coppers' narks', so my brother, Terry, and I had to grow up able to look after ourselves . Everyone used to leave their doors open and people would be in and out of each other's houses all the time. The local bobby was generally a very well-respected figure. I was proud of my dad. He was a very good cop. The house was always full of coppers. The blue uniform ran in our family — our grandfather, Michael, was an Irish copper who was shot dead by the old IRA in the early 1920s. And there was my mum's older brother, also called Michael, who was a mounted policeman in the same Derby force my father joined. In fact, at the time he died my father had just passed his inspector's exams. He used to take me into work quite often. I would go in on his pay-day down to the police station in Full Street. He used to take me into the cells and into the courts. When he became a detective the hours were horrendous. He was away a lot of the time which was why my mother put her foot down in the end. He was very thin as opposed to my shape.

I was the older brother; Terry came along three years later. I think my earliest memory is of Terry being born. I can just recall being taken in the car by my dad to the Nightingale Hospital in Derby. I was told to wait in the back, and a while later he came out again with my mum with a little bundle in her arms. I was given this tiny wriggling thing to hold as we drove back to my granny and grandad's house where we were living at that time. They were looking after me and my dad while my mum was in hospital.

It was such a strange experience. I was delighted to have a little brother and yet it gradually dawned on me that he was invading my territory. We are terribly close, the two of us, but in a separate sort of way. We certainly don't live in each other's pockets but, if either of us need anything or is in any trouble, we are there for each other. When my daughter, Chloe, died, he dropped everything and came to be with me.

I first went to school at Boulton Primary in Alvaston, just near the estate where we lived. I had a lot of illnesses when I was young. First I developed asthma. It was the afternoon after I had my whooping cough jab. Now they recognise the link, but they didn't then. I was quite poorly and I remember my granny leaning over my bed and saying, 'He's going! He's dying!' Even today I carry a Ventolin spray as a stand-by, still suffer from the old wheeze and, if I catch a cold, I have to watch it doesn't turn to bronchitis.

I was desperately keen on sports but I was a very sickly child. I was in the top stream and doing really well at school when I suddenly developed a hip complaint called Perthes Disease. I was only six years old when, for no apparent reason, I just started limping. I didn't even know I wasn't walking properly but people kept commenting. Then one night, I turned over in bed in my sleep and was suddenly woken by a terrible pain. I screamed out in agony but there was nothing to see and my mother took me to the doctor's next morning. They referred me to hospital.

I couldn't understand it. I was really fit and then this mystery illness struck me. Within days of going to the local hospital in Derby, I was taken in to the specialist Bretby Hospital. At first they had no idea what was wrong with me. The X-rays showed there was just a shadow on my hip, but no one seemed to know what was causing it. They thought early on that I had contracted TB because it had similar symptoms. I was actually measured up for the huge cast they used to make for you to treat TB. It was like a coffin and very frightening for an imaginative six year old. But tests showed that it wasn't TB at all.

They still couldn't find out what was wrong so they operated on me and took a piece of my hip-bone away for tests. But there was a strike around that time so instead of it taking a week for the results to come back, it took about five weeks. You can imagine the state my poor mother was in because of that. She was absolutely beside herself.

It was shattering, because I was proud to be the fastest runner in the school at the time. My dad passed on to me his love of sport. He was a very good rugby player, and just missed out on getting into the Welsh national side, and later used to play for Derby Police.

I ended up spending six months of my young life there while they discovered I had this blasted Perthes Disease. It's a condition that hits children when their bodies are still forming. The ball of the hip goes soft and does not fit properly into the hip joint and you therefore develop a limp. The only treatment is still the same now — complete rest. Now I do a lot of work for the Perthes Disease charity, along with Barry Cryer, who must have been a sufferer as well.

I was then in a wheelchair for a year and a half. For three years after that, I couldn't walk without callipers. It was shattering for all my beloved sport to stop and to have to endure the jibes at school. The other kids used to call me Hopalong Cassidy and all sorts of spiteful names. It was horrendous — kids can be very cruel. At playtime, I wasn't allowed to go out and I had to go into a room with one other kid who was disabled.

Being in hospital for six months meant that I missed a lot of schooling. But it did spur me on and toughen me up. When I returned in a calliper, I was bullied something rotten. There was one particular bully called Malcolm Smith who used to push me over. Trapped in the calliper, it was almost impossible to get up on your own. One day it happened again and I went home crying my eyes out. My dad then decided I needed to be able to hit back for myself. He got his old boxing gloves down from the attic and taught me how to box. The next day Malcolm Smith came up calling me Hopalong Cassidy and made as though to push me down, so I put my fists up. He smiled as though it was a joke, but I hit him in the face as hard as I could and I knocked him out cold. So I was a bit of a hero.

The next day, thinking I had just landed a lucky punch, he came back for more to get me back and I knocked him down again. He never came back a third time. I have seen him around since but, strangely, he has always given me a wide berth. We were never exactly friends.

Mercifully, soon afterwards the calliper was removed

and I was determined to pick up where I left off. It wasn't easy because my muscles were very weak through under use. My right leg was terribly withered having not been used for three years — it was an extraordinary feeling. The pain was excruciating and it felt as though I would never be able to walk properly again, let alone run.

But I've always been a determined little blighter and my love of sport dragged me back into action. I wanted so much to be like all the other kids and I was so desperate to play cricket and football that I really pushed myself and trained very hard. I used to go out training with my dad and every chance I got I would be out running to strengthen my legs. And, somehow, by the time I left primary school I was sportsman of the year. I was only supposed to start slowly, walking first a quarter-of-an-hour a day, gradually increasing to half an hour but I ignored that and started with two hours a day at least. By the end of my junior school days, I was in goal for the football team and captain of the cricket team and my memories of the agonies over my legs were fading fast.

But absolutely my worst moment at junior school was being forced to take part in the diving competition in the swimming gala. I got the take-off completely wrong and just fell in. I remember the roars of laughter from 1,000 pupils as I thrashed around underwater. The screams of derision still ring in my ears. I didn't want to come up to face them — it was a nightmare.

My enthusiasm for Derby County goes back to the age of six, when I saw my first match. My dad took me and sat me behind the scoreboard, and I watched the game peering from behind this wooden board on which they used to hang the names of the goalscorers. Bill Curry, the centre forward, was my favourite and there was another hero of mine called George Darwin. I can remember that first match against Bury — we won 4-0. I was hooked for life. Later, we used to go to the boys' pen and you would be passed down over the tops of everyone's heads, finishing on somebody's shoulder. It sounds terribly dangerous in these days of all seater stadiums, but there was no trouble. Derby is a real football town, always was and always will be. I was obsessed by sport as a youngster.

Later, I played for Derby at rugby and cricket, and played football for Heanor Town for one season before I was given a free transfer. Football is part of my life. Even today, there is still a group of about six of us old friends who go to matches together, and that is how we keep in touch with each other. There is Sibbo, Spike, Felix, Rob and Woody. We all go back an awful long way. Sibbo and I are distantly related and have known each other since we were about five. Felix and I went to school together. We meet beforehand, have a few beers and talk about what has happened in the last fortnight. These are guys who have nothing at all to do with showbusiness or television, which is great. One is a legal executive, another works for Rolls Royce, one is unemployed, one is an interpreter and another is in charge of the Derby street cleaners. We're all more or less the same age and they're all a little eccentric. Lesley always used to say she wished I could have 'one normal friend'. But I value their friendship today as much as I ever have done. They don't give a toss that I'm on television.

It is lovely to keep in touch with old friends — they are part of me. That is what is important to me. They mean far more to me than any of the showbiz glamour set that is part and parcel of TV. Some of them are my best friends, people I grew up with from the age of five. I remember at the age of eight crossing the allotments from my house in Alvaston and walking three miles to the football match with one of these mates. You don't forget things like that in a hurry. You couldn't safely let your children do it now, but then my mother never ever worried about us getting back.

Derby County is very close to my heart — it's been a constant factor and one of the most important things in my life. Now I am privileged to count Brian Clough as a friend. In his days at Derby I was just a fan, but what he did was absolutely fantastic, a fairytale come true. I got my opportunity to show my gratitude by appearing on stage with the great man in an evening of his memories in the theatre. Just me and Cloughie on stage and the Derby Playhouse full of football fans. I enjoyed the experience every bit as much as the audience.

I went down from the A stream to the B stream after my time off in hospital, but I soon clawed my way back, passing my 11-plus exam and going to Bemrose Grammar School in Derby. Out of quite a large primary school there were only two boys who passed. My parents were very proud but I was just making up for lost time. It was very posh then — we had to wear smart blazers, and the teachers wore mortar boards, the lot. It was just like being at public school. Not that I cared, I only lived for the sport. It was very strict.

At first, when I heard I had passed I didn't want to go because all my mates were going to the local secondary modern. The first day at Bemrose in my new uniform was pretty terrifying because I didn't know a soul. All the fifth-formers were taking the mickey out of us 120 new boys and I just felt like a fish out of water. There were four classes of 30 in those days. I knew absolutely no one. We were all lined up in alphabetical order and the chap next to me, a lad called Lakin, became a great friend of mine. Once I got to know him it wasn't so bad. I realised we were all as nervous as each other.

There were four houses — Wellington, Sydney, Newton and Burke — appropriately enough, I was put into Burke. The lessons were a bit of a lost cause for me but the games were great. Sport helped me a lot. I have always found it a great way of making friends. Soon, I became house football captain for our year, which made me very popular because I had to pick the team. It was a very early lesson for me on 'how to win friends and influence people'.

My childhood showbusiness hero was Cliff Richard. I thought he was just wonderful. I practised for hours in front of the mirror trying to copy that quiff. I went to the Gaumont in Derby to see Cliff and the Shadows three times when I was a kid and they were great every time. Then I moved on to the Walker Brothers and a little later, of course, The Beatles.

I met the Rolling Stones when I queued up outside the Gaumont with Felix for their autographs. Felix was really into getting autographs. There used to be a café called the Spotlight and, when I was 13, I queued up to get Brian Jones, Bill Wyman and Mick Jagger's autographs. It was brilliant to see them in person. But, by then, the Beatles were still definitely my number-one musical love.

Butlin's was our regular holiday haunt. We went to every single camp and loved them all. It was the working-class family holiday and we thrived on it. And the funny thing is that one of my clearest memories from those days is of Terry nicknaming me Tosh. Prophetic or what? I don't know where he dreamed it up from and it didn't last that long. I have got no idea why. But when we were in Skegness or Filey or Clacton, that was his name for me. It was either that or Fatso.

Academically, I was a dead loss because I seemed to spend all my time in class looking out the window waiting for the next game. I got a report once in which the word 'Scatterbrained' seemed to be on just about every page. My father went absolutely bonkers. In every subject I was criticised, but as a goalkeeper for the soccer team and as a wicketkeeper for the cricket team I did at least get some praise.

I left with a pathetic single 'O'-level in history, my favourite subject, but I only just scraped through that. They say your schooldays are the happiest days of your life and they were for camaraderie and sport, but not, in my case I'm afraid, for learning too much. That is why I always try to drill into my children the importance of working hard at school. I am probably extra strict because I know I wasted a great opportunity. Luckily for me, it didn't matter in the end because of the profession I took up. 'O'-levels don't get you acting work.

I did break one school record but it was for detentions. I just seemed to spend my whole time mucking around — I was a real rebel. I always refused to wear my school cap, which seemed to be almost a hanging offence in those days. The monitors and prefects were the bane of my life. One of them, a great big fellow called McDonald, is now the manager of the Midland Bank, of which I am now a customer. He was always one of the guys who used to give me a hard time, and jokes even to this day that he still does. At least I think he's joking.

The headmaster of the rival school, Derby Grammar, was a chap called Elliott, and his son Nigel was in our year. Nigel was a terribly-terribly posh lad, but a good sportsman all the same. I played rugby and cricket with him and he was captain of both teams. He got on our nerves a lot so, one day, a mate of mine, Charlie Conway, and I threw Nigel's underpants and vest in the shower so they were drenched. It seemed hilarious at the time, but then I can clearly remember the sight of him wandering completely naked down the school corridor, knocking on the staffroom door and saying, 'Lloyd and Conway have thrown my vest and pants in the shower, sir.' Then it wasn't quite so funny. The teacher did not know what to do. Unfortunately, he soon thought of something, and Charlie and I were whisked into the headmaster's office for six of the best. That cane really did hurt.

One year, there was great uproar when somebody climbed the tower and put a bra on the top, but that definitely wasn't me. I was daft but I wasn't stupid. I didn't fancy climbing that tower. I knew who had done it, but we were all sworn to secrecy. I was in 5F and we had a bit of a name as troublemakers.

We had a physics teacher called Holt, and the poor blighter was a nervous wreck. Kids are ruthless in the way they can spot a dodgy teacher and latch on to any sign of weakness for a little fun. The day after John F Kennedy died we decided to have our own three minutes' silence at 12 o'clock, which just happened to be right in the middle of his double physics lesson. He was writing away on the board, talking to us with his back to the class, and we all stood up in silence. He said, 'Right, what is the answer to that, Baker?' and of course we all refused to say a word. We just stood to attention and he went round the class becoming increasingly frustrated at our silence. He used to go round behind people and knuckle them on the back of the head, but that day he had to admit defeat when nobody gave in. He went and asked the headmaster to punish us in the end. When it came to the 'O'-level mock, I managed 1 per cent in physics — I was so bad at it, I even got the boiling temperature of water wrong — and Mr Holt looked pained, simply saying, 'Is it really worth you taking it, Lloyd?' We both quickly agreed that it was not.

The woodwork class was across the street in Albany Road. That was a treble period of an hour-and-a-half and the teachers over there were all nutters. We once turned the clock forward an hour so the lesson ended far too early. He said, 'Time seems to have flown by today, boys.' And, of course, we got done for that as well.

I always had quite a laugh at school. That was where I discovered acting. I wasn't too bad at English and history, but acting was the first thing, apart from sport, for which I seemed to have any aptitude. My stage début was at 12 in a play called *The Case of the Crimson Coconut* in which I played Colonel Arbuthnot. I had a false moustache and I had to come on and park my bike on its stand on the stage. During the first performance, the damn thing fell over. But the audience laughed and I knew straight away that I liked the sound of audience appreciation. I never imagined then I'd ever do it for a living, but I rather liked putting on the make-up and costumes, and I felt the adrenalin pumping when I went out there to face the school halls packed with mums and dads and other kids. It gave me a real buzz. It was the first thing I had found that I was any good at. I did well in the English reading class and won it. That was the first time I stopped larking about in lessons and actually concentrated on something.

I had lots of girlfriends. Bemrose was a boys' school and you got all the usual bragging about exploits with the local girls. But I started quite young — I was 14 when I first went 'all the way' with a girl. Everyone else said they had done it, so I thought it was about time I tried it. Of course, it later turned out their claims were just empty boasts. I was absolutely astonished when I found out I was the first one to do it. That first time was dreadful. It was in a field near where we lived, and a couple out walking their dog came past while we were at it and ruined it all. It was memorable only for its awfulness.

I met her at church of all places, at confirmation classes, and thought she was the sweetest, loveliest little thing I had ever seen. But she was far from innocent even if she looked as though butter wouldn't melt in her mouth. She was quite a bit older than me, and it really was 14 year old fumbling. But she was far more experienced than me. I was just beginning to get the hang of the operation when we heard some voices. This couple were on a summer's evening walk and there was us — starkers. I can just remember jumping up, grabbing my clothes and running like a hare through the long grass. It was terribly embarrassing facing the girl the next time I saw her, and our frenzied passion didn't last much longer.

Later, much later, when I applied for drama school I needed a reference from my old headmaster, Dr W C Chapman (you can guess what his nickname was), even though I had been working in a solicitor's office for years by then. I had to audition for the education committee to try to get a grant. I rang him up full of trepidation thinking that he probably wouldn't remember me. Or, should I say, hoping he wouldn't remember me five years on. I just said, 'It's Lloyd from 5F, sir,' because our 5F was quite famous, or perhaps infamous.

He said, 'Oh yes, I remember you very well. You broke the school record for detentions, how could I forget that? How's the soliciting going?'

'It's not,' I said. 'I've auditioned for drama school and got in. I'm applying for a grant.'

His exact words then knocked me sideways. 'We all knew when you were here that you should have been an actor. I knew, your history teacher knew and your English teacher knew.'

I thought, 'Well, why on earth didn't one of you tell me at the time? I've wasted five years training to be a lawyer.' But he was probably quite right. Acting is a very precarious profession. At least I had a grounding in a sensible career if acting ever rejected me.

It's a sign of how things have changed that I managed to get into a solicitor's office to train to be a solicitor's clerk with my single 'O'-level on the understanding that I went to night school and got 'O'-level English. I don't think that would happen today.

My father was strict and a bit disappointed at my lack of academic progress, but my mum was so flabbergasted that I had got into grammar school in the first place that she didn't worry too much. It was a great achievement after I had missed so much work because of my illness. Only two boys and two girls managed to get places at the grammar school that year. But in all my time at Bemrose, the highest I came was 25th out of 29 in the bottom group, so I wasn't exactly a high flier.

CHAPTER TWO

LLOYD THE LAWYER

When I left school at 16 with my single 'O'-level, I did think of following my father into the police force. My dad had helped me a lot and, like all good parents, he wanted me to have a better upbringing and life than he had had himself. He encouraged me to become either a journalist, a solicitor or an accountant. And he helped me to get interviews for jobs in all three professions. I thought I might have to be able to write to become a journalist and to add up to become an accountant, so, after due deliberation, I chose to try to become a solicitor. But I'm afraid I had no vocation in the legal sphere. I joined Taylor, Simpson and Mosley in St Mary's Gate, Derby, and it didn't take me very long to realise that it just wasn't for me. I have always been a very jovial, up-beat sort of bloke who loves to have a joke, and a solicitors' office is not exactly a laugh a minute. It was like going back to the days of Scrooge, with dingy, dark old offices covered in cobwebs.

In many ways it was an interesting firm. The boss was called Grimwood Taylor, and he was as bald as a coot because he lost all his hair during the First World War. He was a very frightening figure to a young lad who has just come out of school. He certainly terrified me. I was instructed that I had to wear a smart, three-piece suit every day — again, it was Dickensian, rather like stepping back into the last century.

There was a big boardroom which, for some reason, had a suit of armour on display. I was always in trouble because I was frequently late for work. I used to try to creep in through the back door, dump my coat somewhere, grab a file and just walk through as if I'd been there since dawn. I used to receive constant reprimands for having long hair and growing a beard. But it certainly opened my eyes — I was doing divorces at the age of 17. And I prepared the defence on three murder cases which certainly makes you grow up in a hurry. My personal boss was a chap called Robert Heelis, who ended up as the Sheriff of Derby.

One Saturday night, my friends and I were out on the town in Derby on our way to a party in Normanton when we came across a scene of terrific police activity. Three people had been killed in a bitter dispute between two Indian families. It was outside the Cambridge Hotel near the Baseball Ground. They had been stabbed to death and there was blood everywhere. I was shocked, and spotted one of my father's police mates. He said darkly, 'You'd better move on, young Taff, this is a really bad one.' I didn't really give it another thought. Then, on the Monday morning, I was sent into the police station to interview three of the five men accused of those dreadful killings. I was only 19 and I don't mind admitting that I was terrified.

There used to be a pub opposite there. I went for a drink before I went in to interview the Singhs, the family accused of murder. The coppers knew me because of my dad and showed me into the cell. One of them said, 'When you've finished, Taff, ring the bell. But I've got to lock the door because of security.' It was a tiny room with just one small window, and I suffer from claustrophobia. It was awful and I was in there for about an hour-and-a-half.

Naturally, they all fiercely denied the murders. They reckoned they were in Wolverhampton at the time. I was so relieved when it was over and I rang the bell, but there was no answer. I could feel the panic and the sweat start to rise in me. I was locked in a room with three murderers. We ended up talking about the weather, how Derby County were doing, just about anything to pass the time. I was a complete nervous wreck by the time the copper returned 25 minutes later. 'I just thought I'd have a quick cuppa,' he said cheerily.

I was so shaken I went straight back to the pub and had another couple of pints. Their alibis were completely false, of course, so I had to go and see them again in Leicester nick, although at least there were guards around us then. They gave me different stories that time. The case went on and on and I left to go to drama school before it came to court but, as I had prepared the defence, I followed it through and found that they were all as guilty as Hell — one went down for life, one for nine years and one for eleven. They had organised a get-together and then ambushed and stabbed their victims through the neck — and I had been left locked in a room with these charmers for 25 minutes.

I have so many happy memories of my teenage years. Socially, my life really took off once I managed to get behind the wheel of a car. It took me three attempts to pass my driving test, which was embarrassing for both me and my dad as he was teaching me. I don't think he was that impressed by my driving because I was always a bit speedy. I have always tried to do everything quickly, not just driving — that's just the way I am. I passed my test at the third attempt and I was so used to the examiner saying, 'Oh, I'm sorry, you've failed,' that when he turned to me and said, 'You've passed,' I was completely freaked out by it. I passed in my dad's motor, a maroon Ford Cortina. It was a great car and I really had some fun in it. Especially in the back seat.

I'm afraid I wasn't always a very careful driver. I once took a load of people home late after a night out. We had three in the front and four in the back so the car was pretty overloaded, but this was long before drink-driving breathalyser days, thank goodness. I took them all home from a club in Derby, and there is a tree in Chaddesden just opposite the graveyard that still bears the scars from where I overshot the bend that night. I was going much too fast, of course. Everyone got slowly out of the car shaking their heads and, mercifully, we gradually realised that no one was seriously hurt. Then... disaster! A man rushed out of a nearby house and said breathlessly, 'It's all right, I've rung the police, they'll be here in a minute.'

I thought, 'Terrific!' I sent my dazed passengers running off before the boys in blue arrived and then, being a very naughty lad at the time, I struggled to

20

reverse the car out of the tree to get away before the police came. But it was stuck fast and very soon a stroppy copper arrived. He was filling out the inevitable charge sheet.

'Name?'

'Lloyd, Kevin Reardon.'

'Occupation of father?'

'Policeman.'

'You're not Taffy Lloyd's son are you?'

'Yes,' I admitted with a heavy heart. I knew that my father would not be impressed. He sighed and screwed up the charge sheet.

'Right,' he said, and I said something not very nice and he replied, 'In that case I'm not going to do you, I'm going to do something a lot worse. I'm going to tell your father, he'll give you better punishment.'

Being a cocky 18-year-old, I said, 'Well, get stuffed and get on with it.' He was quite considerate in the circumstances and, despite my cheek, he helped me remove the car from the tree and drive home. I slipped up to bed thinking that perhaps it had all been forgotten about, then at two or three o'clock in the morning I was rudely awoken by my father in full Sergeant's uniform.

He ordered me downstairs to the kitchen. When I walked in, he said, 'Did you have a crash tonight?'

'Yes, Dad.'

'Did you run into a tree?'

'Yes, Dad.'

'Did you cheek the police officer who attended?'

I said, 'Yes, Dad.'

'Right,' he said, 'I admire your honesty.'

And then whack! he slapped me one that knocked me right across the kitchen. It didn't half hurt. It bloody hurt because my old man was an ex-boxer but I think he was absolutely right as a dad. He said to me, 'Had you been dishonest, you would have got two clouts.'

He was right, but I'm afraid even that shock treatment didn't improve my driving. Once my red Mini had been repaired, it went on to become famous in Derby because it had more crashes than any other car in the city.

I never drank until I was 18. It was a lot stricter then and I think that being the son of a policeman helped to keep me on the straight and narrow. Now I am appalled if my 16-year-old son tells me that he has been out and had a pint of beer. In my time, to drink before you were 18 was completely out of order. I never did it. But when I was 18, I went to the Locarno in Derby and, trying to be flash with my Beatle haircut and Beatle jacket, I thought I was really Jack-the-lad, I had a lot to drink and started chatting up some girl who thought I was a complete idiot. When I got home, my bedroom was spinning round like there was no tomorrow.

I was sick in the bathroom and then sick in my bedroom, and I remember my mother coming in and saying, 'What do you think you are doing?' I got a slap across the face and next morning, with a raging hangover, I was ordered to get down on my knees and clean the sick up. I am far from proud to recall that that happened quite a few times. But I learned my lesson eventually.

In those days, I was very proud of my hair, even if most of it has gone now. I find it hard to believe now that it used to take me hours to prepare the most elaborate quiff. I was almost pleased when it went out of fashion — thank goodness I could have a Beatle cut and save time.

I have always been a bit shy, but I seemed to manage to attract girlfriends. My schoolfriends even used to say

I was the man for the girls. I always had a pretty good sense of humour and remember this being a long time before my fat days. But getting off with girls could be a difficult business. I actually had a friend with the alarming name of Rob Novitt, and one night at the Locarno we spotted a couple of likely looking ladies on the dance floor, 'Let's go and chat these two birds up,' I said.

I wandered up to them, imagining I looked exactly like Cliff Richard in *Expresso Bongo*, and said, 'Me and my friend want to dance with you and your friend.'

The girl looked surprised and said 'What friend is that, then?'

I looked round to see that although Rob had come in with me, his nerves had presumably got the better of him and he'd legged it. Of course, everyone knows you can get nowhere with two girls.

That was embarrassing, but I think the most hurtful thing that happened was after I had been out with another girl about two or three times and she had said, 'We'll go to the pictures. Can you bring a friend for my friend?' So I asked my pal, Kevin Ryan, whose nickname was Felix because there were two Kevins in our gang, if he would come and make up the foursome.

The night came and he let me down — he never showed. I had to go and meet these two very attractive girls in the marketplace in town. I was dreading it, because you can't snog with more than one girl, at least, I couldn't imagine it happening in those days. They seemed to accept the idea of me accompanying them alone, but then we all wanted to go to the toilets. I went down to the Gents and they went to the Ladies. I came out and I waited for them... and I waited... and I waited. Eventually, the penny dropped — they had done a bunk. I was absolutely heart-broken. I couldn't believe anybody could be so rude as to do that to me, and I didn't half give Felix a piece of my mind when I finally tracked him down.

I had some successes with girls as well, but there were plenty of times when girls have turned me down. There's nothing more crushing than rejection. When you say to a girl, 'Do you fancy a dance?' and she answers, 'No, not with you,' it makes you feel about an inch tall.

For someone in their late teens being a solicitor's clerk can be a very educational job. I had a girl who came in to the office once wanting a divorce, and I knew from my times spent out on the town that she was the Derby bike. Just about every lad I knew had been there. At that time, you had to get the female petitioner to sign a form swearing that 'During my marriage, I have not had sexual intercourse with any person other than my husband.' It was the law then. I knew her and she knew that I knew her, and when it came to the embarrassing point of getting this piece of paper out, she read it, looked me straight in the eye and said, 'What exactly is sexual intercourse?' I opened a dictionary and read the definition: 'Penetration with the male organ ...' and she said, 'Oh well you don't mean fingers, then,' and she signed it. The law moves in mysterious ways. She still somehow managed to be six months pregnant with another bloke's baby when she got her divorce.

One of the first cases I was given to handle was that of a middle-aged lady, a tiny wisp of a woman who looked as though she wouldn't say 'boo' to a goose. She was up for shoplifting and, crying her eyes out, she told me the heart-rending story of her life and how her husband would kill her if he found out the trouble she was in. I felt desperately sorry for her and started trying to figure out if there was some way in which I could prevent the injustice of her having to go to court. I was passionate then — I was even quite good, everybody said so. I thought I was at least the next Perry Mason, and I was totally convinced by this lady as I started to prepare an action against the police.

How on earth could they arrest such a charming and clearly innocent woman, accuse her of such an embarrassing offence and make her cry? It was blindingly obvious she did not do it. We went to court and I worked my socks off. But my confidence began to wane a little when a copper mate of my dad's said, 'You'll learn, Taff,' and laughed. I was totally convinced that my client was innocent, and I started accusing him of having made a mistake. Of course, when the case was heard she was found guilty. I was shocked. And when her antecedents were read out and it took about a quarter-of-an-hour, I was even more shocked. She had a record as a thief as long as your arm. I felt so small coming out of that courtroom, but that friend of my father's was quite right. I did learn my lesson. I was never quite so trusting again, and there were no tears afterwards from the woman. She was as guilty as sin, and I had really thought that a major injustice had been done.

Life was often funny in my days as a trainee solicitor. I used to muck about most of the time and, with my long hair and beard, I became very much the office rebel. We had a very pretty receptionist called Marion. Downstairs, where they kept all the files, there was a spooky cellar, which was said to be haunted. Mountains of cases, each neatly wrapped up in red ribbon, were stored in the dusty old room that looked exactly like something from a Hammer horror film. Marion was very young and attractive, and she was also terrified of ghosts. So as an initiation to the firm, we decided to set her up.

There was a little alcove down there behind the door and my mate, Arthur Titterton, sent her down to look for a file. I had already slipped into the alcove and remained hidden in the pitch-black room. She came down very tentatively because she never liked visiting the cellar. As she moved past me, I slowly pushed out a file in her direction. It appeared mysteriously from nowhere as if by some supernatural force. You could hear the screams for what seemed like ages as she raced right through the building. Unfortunately, I did get into serious trouble because the senior partners came down to investigate and I was still in my hiding place waiting for a chance to slip out unnoticed. I got a real rollicking for that.

I know it doesn't sound very modest but I had lots of girlfriends. I liked girls and they seemed to like me. I put my early success down to my cheeky charm and youthful good looks. It was the era of the mods and rockers, and I was very definitely a mod, one of Derby's finest. I had a scooter and a full-length leather jacket, and I thought I was the bee's knees.

The girls were all great fun, but none of them was remotely serious until I met Hilary Jennings. She was different. She arrived at work as the new receptionist after Marion's departure and I was immediately attracted. Before Hilary, they were all very quick affairs, kissing on the back seat at the pictures and then trying to go further later on. Hilary was not like that at all. She was a lady. I thought I was Jack-the-lad, immune from ever really falling in love, but as soon as I met Hilary I fell really heavily, head-over-heels in love straight away.

We met at work. When I was first introduced to her she just took my breath away. My mouth opened but nothing came out. She was very pretty and very shy. I think, at first, she thought I was arrogant and blasé with a reputation for having a string of local girls. I think she decided she wasn't going to be just another conquest and was quite cool with me. But we were both attracted to each other and one night at a dance in The Grandstand pub at Derbyshire Cricket Ground, it just sort of happened. We started dancing and when the music stopped we didn't want to let go of each other, and we ended up kissing. It was magical. I felt as though I was floating on air for the rest of the night. I just couldn't believe it was happening to me, I almost had to pinch myself to make sure I wasn't dreaming. But even then she was very determined she was not going to be just another notch on my bedstead, which she wasn't. I realised quite quickly that she was very special.

Hilary swept me off my feet. I was just 17 and used to getting girls into bed quickly, but she made me wait until we were both properly ready. It was completely different with her to anything I had experienced before. We talked endlessly and laughed at all the same things. I felt for months that I was in paradise. Our colleagues at work soon found out, of course, but that wasn't a problem. I think they thought it was very sweet, two young co-workers falling for each other like that. It was a pure, innocent romance. We were very much in love. She was perfectly behaved and discreet, and she changed my life completely. I went from really playing the field to never looking at another woman while I was going out with Hilary.

Hilary was beautiful. She looked a little bit like a blonde version of a young Rita Tushingham. I have always preferred blondes, like a lot of gentlemen. She was just extremely feminine. She was very quiet and shy, very slim, just a couple of inches shorter than me. I felt we were made for each other. She was lovely, absolutely gorgeous and very much a lady. I first met her when she was brought round and introduced to us as the new solicitors' receptionist. And she stopped me in my tracks straight away. That ended all my playing around. She was more than a bit special.

One of my fondest memories of Hilary is when I bought her a kilt for Christmas. At the time, neither of us had much money but we were blissfully happy and were definitely going to get married. That Christmas, I knew that she really wanted a particular smart, kilt-style skirt. It was very expensive, or seemed so at the time. But I had worked hard to save up enough money to get her this skirt. I can remember very clearly to this day how her eyes sparkled on Christmas Day when she unwrapped this kilt. She was absolutely delighted. It was beautiful. It was the perfect present. It still rates as the best gift I have given anybody because I knew how much it meant to her. She was a beautiful person and was very, very important to me. It's nearly 30 years ago since she unwrapped that kilt but I still treasure that moment.

Before Hilary, I was just like most other 16- or 17-year-old lads, trying to go out at the weekends and get off with a girl. Suddenly, Hilary changed all that. I didn't want to go out and try to score all the time.

I am very romantically inclined, and liked to treat Hilary well. Romance means a lot to me. Girls did take to me when I was younger, but I learned then that I was really a one-woman man. At first, Hilary and I had hardly any money because, although we were both working, all the stories you have heard about lawyers being mean with their money were true when it came to paying wages. Our nights were spent mainly round at our parents' houses. One of our first serious dates was at the Pavilion at Matlock Bath, where we went to dance and got the bus back to Derby. I must have been very much in love with her because I walked her all the way home to Chaddesden, about four miles. I was so protective I wouldn't let her walk on her own or get a taxi, so I walked with her all the way, arrived there at about two o'clock in the morning, and then I walked all the way back to my home in Alvaston.

I think being with Hilary helped to take my mind off how excruciatingly dull the job had become. Towards the end of my time there, I could speak up in registrar's chambers and in magistrates courts, something which I enjoyed enormously, but it was usually barristers or qualified solicitors who held the floor. I was generally left to do the tedious preparation work. I never imagined at the time that all this was excellent training for my time as an actor in *The Bill*. I was working with the police, meeting all the criminals and, as an added bonus, I got to know some of the hardest blokes in Derby.

There was one case which should have gone down in history — my father was the prosecuting policeman, I was the defence solicitor's clerk and my brother was the journalist reporting on the case. So all three of us were in action in Derby Magistrates Court in Full Street. It was a robbery of some kind, with me fighting my dad in court and my brother reporting on it. We had a good laugh about that afterwards. And my dad won, as he usually did.

But it gradually dawned on me that I was trapped in a

life I didn't want. I am not proud of breaking up with Hilary, but it seemed the only thing I could do at the time. And I did tell her to her face. I made the decision up a big hill in Chaddesden, a local beauty spot. I was up there one day with a mate of mine who was just back from university, and I realised I absolutely hated working at the solicitors. It just wasn't me. It was so boring. I was into amateur dramatics and everyone was saying, 'You should go to drama school,' and I first thought you had to be different to act for a living, not someone ordinary like me. I was thinking about my mate's free and easy life at college with the world before him, and I started to think about me in that solicitor's office every day of the week.

I could see my life behind a desk stretching ahead of me with the odd excursion to the courts and I definitely didn't like what I saw. I decided there and then that I had to try drama school, even if I failed I knew I would never be happy unless I tried. So I went back and told Hilary I had decided I was going to go away and I felt I had to leave everything, all my ties with the past. I just felt I had to get away from Derby completely.

Both sets of parents wanted us to marry. We had almost become unofficially engaged. My mother was dreadfully upset when it finished and never really took to anybody else. Hilary had become part of the family, almost like a daughter.

But if breaking up with Hilary was one emotional blow, an even greater one was about to come. My father was killed in a car crash. He was rushing to answer an emergency call when the police car skidded on black ice. With the cruellest irony imaginable, it turned out to be a false alarm triggered by the bad weather. I was very close to my father. He was a wonderful man and when he died it was the worst thing that had ever happened to me. He died so suddenly, and I don't believe that my mother ever got over the shock. I can still clearly remember her horrible screams when she was told what had happened. It was Terry, or Tes as I call him, who came into my room and broke the awful news to me.

I was left with great regrets about all the things I did not say or do. I wish we had been closer at the time he died. I was 20 and very unhappy in my job. I was still living at home, although I had left a couple of times because of family friction. You do a lot of daft things at that age. I hated my work, and I had just gone through a traumatic split with Hilary. I had left home twice, and moved into different places in Derby. And then my dad was taken away so suddenly at a time when we weren't getting on as well as we should have done. I still wish I'd had the chance to tell him how much I loved him.

I am sure we would have become close again. I wish he had had the opportunity see me happy and successful in my work, and I know he would have deeply loved all the grandchildren. I have always regretted that he had never known that I became an actor. I also think he would have loved *The Bill*. He knew before he died that I was considering a move to become an actor, and that I was trying to get into drama school. He wasn't too pleased about the idea at first. For one thing, he thought all actors were poofs. He was a tough Welsh rugby player and he reckoned you had to be homosexual to dress up in tights and prance around on stage.

But he was so caring and thoughtful, being a copper he naturally decided to make a few enquiries for himself. I had to be very determined because he was dead set against it. He wanted me to become a solicitor and go to work in my pin-stripe suit. When I won the chance of a place at East 15 drama school, he asked somebody on the education committee about drama schools, and they said, 'If he gets in he's got talent, but the odds are still stacked against him.'

One of the last conversations I ever had with my father before he died was about this. He said, 'I have made enquiries and if you do get into drama school, you can go with my blessing. I will back you to the hilt.' I have remembered that to this day. And that is what kept my mother going, the fact that my father recognised that if I got in somewhere, I must have some talent because of the competition. I would have gone anyway because I was so determined, but it would have been a terrible family wrench and it meant a great deal to me to get his blessing. It still does. My father died in the February just after I had been for the auditions to drama school. I only heard that I had got in after he had died.

Everything seemed to happen at once. I was 21 on 28 March 1970, and, as I reached that magical age, I was suffering a real inner turmoil. I was devastated by my father dying, guilty about jilting Hilary and still not totally sure that I had done the right thing in giving up a secure, if boring, career for the chance of going to drama school. Somehow, my determination to make it as an actor was forged at this time, even if I did not even begin to realise it until later. I think my mother would have liked me to stay behind, but the decision had been taken by then. I just knew that this was my chance and that I had to take it.

I will always regret that I was not able to share my success with my dad. He was typical of most policemen, brave and decent and hard-working. The police are much maligned these days and they don't get the backing they deserve. Of course, there are rotten apples in every barrel, but with the police it is all blown up out of proportion. It is very fashionable to knock the force but, usually, the people who criticise the loudest are the first ones to dial 999 when they are in trouble.

Leaving the solicitors' office was a decision I have never regretted. I was sitting behind a desk filling in forms, and I could see myself still being behind that desk at 45, wishing to goodness I had done something more exciting with my life. I kept saying that to myself. Some are still there. The chap that I worked with, Arthur Titterton, is now a solicitor with his own business. Some of the old boys have died and a lot have retired. It cost me a huge drop in income but the money was not important to me. When I left, I was earning £35 a week as a litigation clerk and I had to get used to living on a £12-a-week grant, including my £3-a-week scholarship.

CHAPTER THREE

LLOYD THE ACTOR

I wanted to go to drama school very much, but I was very apprehensive. I thought I would find myself in a class of 44 Laurence Oliviers and one Kevin Lloyd. I was the awkward young lad from Derby, and I fully expected to stand out like a sore thumb. When I received the acceptance from drama school, my mother was shocked. She did not think I would get in and I am sure she hoped I wouldn't be accepted. I had only been to London to watch football matches before, and I organised the move all myself, even down to finding somewhere to live. The drama school was in East London, Loughton, Essex. I booked in for a week at a bed and breakfast place. When I got there in October 1970, I found loads of us looking for somewhere to live and four of us joined forces and rented a flat together.

Right from the start, being at drama school gave me an amazing feeling of freedom. For the first time in my life, I felt I became what I was supposed to be, I had found my destiny if you like, if people from Derby can have a destiny. To do that, I knew I had to part from Hilary, otherwise I think I might be with her today. I knew I had to follow it through on my own. I knew I had done the right thing as soon as I got on the train at Derby. I had not travelled much, and going to London then was like my son, Mark, going to live in New York now. My mother was terrified of what was going to happen to me. I didn't know what to expect but I knew it was a big, big step and loads of friends have said to me since, 'My God, I wish I had done what you did.' But I believe if you want something, you have got to go after it. Otherwise, I would still be in that solicitors' office today. My life would have been all planned out before me, and I just couldn't face it.

My mum never believed I was going until I packed my solitary case that Sunday morning. I had my belongings in my bag and my heart in my mouth. To make matters worse, I was almost as overweight then as I am now. I feared it was all going to be disastrous. What on earth was a fat lad from Derby doing thinking he could act?

The first day at East 15 was quite terrifying. There were 45 of us in that intake and we were all shepherded into the theatre and given the bad news. There was to be no gentle introduction, no chance to sit at the back and get to know the ropes gradually. We each had to do a Shakespeare piece, a modern piece, a comedy, a poem, a song and a dance — in front of all the others. Looking back, I think the powers that be at East 15 were quite mean to inflict that ordeal on a load of nervous new boys and girls. Fortunately, we had to do it in alphabetical order so, being an 'L', I was in the middle. I was able to see some people before me who, I was delighted to see, were pretty ordinary and I knew I wasn't quite that bad. That gave me a bit of confidence. I thought, 'At least I can match that.' They definitely weren't all Laurence Olivier.

I've always thought it was a bit unfair because we were judged and graded for our future on our first morning when most of us were still feeling lost and homesick.

My Shakespeare was a speech from *Richard II*, I followed it with a speech from *Little Malcolm and his Struggle Against the Eunuchs* by David Halliwell, which was very popular at the time. It was all the rage, partly because it was full of good audition speeches. Slowly, I began to warm up and almost enjoy myself. I did a dance routine. I'd had a couple of dance lessons, but I'm not a dancer, I tend to move like a rugby player who is well into the after-match celebrations. I sang a song from *Oh, What A Lovely War*. I can remember it all clearly. I felt terrified as my turn approached but, gradually, I realised that everyone else was just as nervous and it wasn't too bad.

After that first day, we were all graded A, B, C, or D. It seemed a bit like going into a secondary school. I thought it was terribly harsh because, if you were labelled a D, it was pretty obvious you hadn't got much of a future, and the first day of the course seemed rather soon to be writing people off. I was graded a B and there were quite a few Americans there who seemed to make up most of the As. They were very good at all the singing and dancing as Yanks often are.

By the end of my first year, I had done well and managed to grab quite a few good parts, so, somehow, without wanting to blow my own trumpet too hard, I was emerging as a top dog. We performed a play called *Fuente Ovejuna* by Lorca about the Spanish Revolution and it went really well. In the third year, Joan Littlewood herself picked me out for some great projects and I even got to play the infamous title role in the final production of *Macbeth*. Tony Scannell, who was later to serve alongside me in Sun Hill CID, was carrying a spear. I don't think he ever forgave me.

The four-week run of *Macbeth* was packed throughout. But as so often with this particular play, some strange things happened. Two weeks into the run, the lad playing Seton broke his wrist so we had to get a first-year called Jon Miller to take over. He was a very tall, good-looking, gay Australian. He had a beautiful voice and he was a striking lad. On his opening night he was a bit nervous. There's a point in the play where Macbeth has a long soliloquy and then you hear the scream of Lady Macbeth offstage. As Macbeth, I had to say, 'Seton, find out what that noise is.' Then I go into another soliloquy and as the play is building to its dramatic climax, Seton comes back and I say, 'Seton, wherefore was that noise?' He is supposed to reply, 'The Queen, my lord, is dead.' It's the crux of the whole play.

On his opening night, however, the Australian came to his big moment, looked me straight in the eye, and enunciated expertly: 'My wife, your lord, is dead.' And for a second or two, you could have heard a pin drop. I was so close to saying, 'There's a lot of it about,' but I just managed to keep my wits about me and said, 'What about my wife, Seton?' And he replied, 'Ooooooh. She's dead, too.'

The uproar of laughter was deafening, and I had to go into yet another serious soliloquy with the rest of my year and most of the audience in hysterics. I'm a terrible giggler, and the only way I could stop myself laughing was by using sheer anger, so when I went into the fight scene which followed, I went right over the top which surprised the first actor I had to tackle because I booted him so hard between the legs that he never quite knew what hit him.

Socially, life was rather like something out of *Men Behaving Badly*. When the great Albert Finney was asked, 'What did drama school do for you?' he answered that it completed his sex education. And, I have to say, I couldn't agree more.

Something clicked with me even after that first day. I grew a beard and I threw myself into the freedom of it all. I became a student. It was such a relief not to be wearing the shirt and tie, and the dreaded three-piece striped suit from my soliciting days. It was wonderful to be scruffy and relaxed. We had movement classes and I lost three stone in three months, not through dieting, just by being fitter and happier. It was a wonderfully overwhelming sense of freedom. It was almost as if I had just come out of prison. I thought it was sensational. I had found what I had been looking for without ever really knowing what it was. I just loved it. Not that it wasn't long hours and hard work. We worked seven days a week at East 15, but it never seemed like hard work. We were all together with a common goal, and when you're young and enthusiastic and aiming for the stars, the sky is the limit.

At the end of the first term, four of us, three blokes and a girl, found a flat in Chingford. It was rather like *The Young Ones*, only a little more squalid. Corinna, our resident female, was very understanding of all the laddish behaviour. When she went to have a bath, naturally I used to climb up on somebody's shoulders to look in. Sophisticated we were not, but I think she came to love us in the end. Strangely, actors had such a terrible reputation that we only got the flat because we pretended we were medical students.

Anything went in those free and easy days, and I wouldn't have missed them for the world. The 1960s might have been over, but we were keen to extend the era of free love for as long as possible. One night, we had been out drinking and we came back to find one couple, Andy and his very attractive girlfriend, fast asleep in the lounge. She seemed to quite like me and I couldn't resist giving her a goodnight kiss while Andy was lying asleep next to her. She woke up with a jerk, you might say, and suddenly we were snogging away. Andy woke up half-way through and thought it was a bad dream. She wrote to me some years later when I got *The Bill* and said 'Do you remember that night?' Nothing more happened, but it was a bit naughty. That was *Men Behaving Badly*.

Another very strange character at East 15 was a guy called Martin von Hasselburg who invented the smallest theatre in the world. He used to do performances in the back of his own London taxi which he had bought specially. He wanted me to join his tiny troupe, but I declined. That was avant garde theatre that did not do a lot for me. Martin now calls himself Harry Kipper and has become Mr Bette Midler, but I still think I made the right decision to turn him down to aim at rather larger stages.

Ruby Wax was also at East 15 — she was always at the parties and even then she was very, very loud. She didn't seem to like being at drama school at all, but she was very confident. Billy Murray, now better known as Sergeant Beech from *The Bill*, went to East 15 but he was there before me. Oliver Tobias was a former student and he used to come back and drive his Mini Moke all over the playing fields just in case anyone forgot him. We had a lake there and, if you were one of the unlucky ones, you were thrown in it. It was a sort of initiation ceremony. I was thrown in once and it was very, very cold.

I lived with a girl called Louise who was a stage manager at the drama school. We met up in my third year and were together for a year-and-a-half. Her parents lived at Shipston-on-Stour so we sometimes used that as a base to go to Stratford to watch Shakespeare. She eventually went on to the RSC and I went to Manchester and the relationship petered out.

I did have flings with actresses but I never wanted them to develop into long-term relationships. There was always too much ego in the way with two actors. I don't think I'm too bad as far as an ego is concerned, but I've got enough and I'm aware of it. Relationships between actors must be very hard work. Imagine if you're both out of work at the same time or, even worse, if she's working and you're not. Crikey.

It's great fun at drama school but the failure rate is frighteningly high. Out of the 45 of us who started in my year, I think only 11 graduated. And of those only about four, me, Janine Duvitski and a couple of others — made it. It's a very hard business in which to earn a living. Would-be actors and actresses should always be aware that they are trying to find work in one of the most difficult professions there is. It seems dead easy from the outside, but I've seen plenty of talented people fall by the wayside.

Apart from that one night, that final production of *Macbeth* seemed to go very well. In any case, I received four separate offers of work. I quickly agreed to go up to Burnley but then received an even more tempting offer from Alan Dossor at the Liverpool Everyman. I had to fulfil my commitment to Burnley first, and then I had signed a contract to do a play in Manchester at the Library Theatre. The film star, Anthony Hopkins, was up there in the city, then filming *War and Peace* at Granada. We were doing *Richard II* and he had a friend called Michael Hayward who was appearing in it, so he came over to see it. This was very much during his so-called 'hell-raising' days, and we met him in the bar afterwards.

He seemed a very nice bloke. We all went to a party afterwards and we had to stop on the way for him to get two bottles of whisky, one for the party and one for him. Half-way through the evening, he really got into the swing of things and started doing impressions. He is a wonderful mimic and began by taking off Laurence Olivier, John Gielgud and Ralph Richardson. I then chipped in with my silly Norman Wisdom routine. Almost as soon as I had said, 'Morning, Mr Grimsdale,' he literally grabbed me, took me off into another room and locked the door.

Isn't it funny the things that happen when you've had a drink? I thought, 'Oh my God, it's true what they say. All actors really are poofs.' But he sat me down, stared at me intently and said, 'I'll give you Olivier, Richardson and Gielgud, if you will give me Norman Wisdom.' He was suddenly deadly serious and we were in that room for about an hour swapping impressions. That's how drunk we were, talking in these ridiculous voices. He found it almost impossible because that marvellous Welsh voice of his is so deep, but he got it in the end and he was delighted. I'm told it is still part of his party routine.

Richard Griffiths, who went on to star in *Pie in the Sky*, was up there with me in *Richard II*, which was a riot of a production. I was playing Young Hotspur and one afternoon, before a matinée, I had washed my hair, and for some reason it was sticking up on end which gave me the appearance of a startled cockatoo. There was one scene between Hotspur, the Duke of York, played by Richard, and Bolingbroke, who was played by Alan Moore. A party of schoolchildren were in the audience and both Richard and Alan were concerned that we would not be able to get through it with my hair in this alarming state. I whispered in the wings, 'I can't do anything about it.' When we got on stage, my worst fears were realised because a group of schoolgirls just became hysterical with laughter when they saw my hair. We had to do the plotting scene. Richard Griffiths had a speech that started 'Tut tut', and that was all he could get out before choking with laughter. Alan Moore was even worse. He was dressed in armour and a trickle started leaking out of the bottom. He was pissing himself in every sense of the word.

After my spell in Manchester, I moved on to the most exciting theatre in the most exciting city in the world at the time. I thought I already knew how to enjoy myself, but when I experienced life in Liverpool I realised that I had hardly started. It was fabulous.

I went up on the train from Derby and my mother was terrified all over again because she had heard horrible things about Liverpool being really rough and full of fighting seamen. I wasn't frightened but I was apprehensive, yet it turned out to be one of the most enjoyable periods of my life. I had a year-and-a-bit among the Scousers and I loved every minute.

I just got off the train at Lime Street and asked somebody where the theatre was. I walked up to Hope Street and my first impression was pretty disappointing. The building looked dilapidated and I soon found out that it was even worse inside. You had to share the dressing-rooms with rats. But it had a marvellous bistro where everybody met, such as all the Scaffold, and the Liverpool poets, Adrian Henry and Bryan Patten.

The actors there at the time became great friends, almost from day one. There was Geoff Durham, who went on to become the magician 'The Great Soprendo', and his best trick was marrying Victoria Wood. He was a hopeful young actor doing children's theatre. We had that fine thespian Bill Nighy and the talented Nicholas Woodason, now a leading light at the Royal Shakespeare Company, and a young actress called Julie Walters. Nick Stringer joined me then and much later in *The Bill* playing Sergeant Smollet.

The Liverpool Everyman was the best company I have ever worked with, without a shadow of a doubt. It was brave and inventive and only interested in the very highest standards of performance. *The Bill* is similar but in a rather more grown-up way. Alan Dossor was the director then, but when I arrived he had gone away on a sabbatical and the great Jonathan Pryce, the actor, was standing in as artistic director for the first six months. Alan chose the company and had cast most of it, but Pryce was left to direct *The Taming of the Shrew*.

Before that production got under way, some of the young and enthusiastic newcomers were dispatched to try our hand at street theatre. It was the first time I'd ever attempted to entertain the public that close up and it was certainly very different from working in the cosy and formal atmosphere of a theatre. We did a show that revolved around the unlikely premise of one actor playing a Green Monster inside a large and colourful costume, and the rest of us rounding up an audience of people to play games with him. In the well-behaved, middle-class outposts like Southport and Crosby, it worked well enough. Then some genius decided that we should try working in that famous Liverpool over-spill town of Kirkby. Beirut would probably have been more welcoming.

We must have been bloody mad. We were just sent out and we had to take it in turns to be the Green Monster. It was during the school summer holidays and we would set off in the van with Bill Nighy at the wheel. Nicholas Woodeson was disguised as the Monster and the rest of us rushed around drumming up indifference among the locals.

Nicholas was deposited on an open bit of land nearby, waiting for the show to start. Being Liverpudlians, the citizens of Kirkby were mainly very quick-witted, and often in answer to the question, 'Have you seen the Green Monster?' they would reply, quick as a flash, 'Yes, the wife's at the supermarket right now.'

The plan was to attract the kids in and organise games with them. It was very hard playing the Green Monster, you used to sweat buckets in a hideous costume that was sweltering even on an ordinary day, but when the weather warmed up, you boiled.

Kirkby is a very tough area and the 'lads' soon arrived to join in the fun. I'm all for audience participation, but this lot began with the odd brick and worked their way up to more serious ammunition. In the end we had to run for it. They weren't going to play any games. Unfortunately, hapless Nicholas in the Green Monster's outfit couldn't run very fast, but Bill Nighy and I made a sharp exit as bricks and debris flew round our ears. We eventually reached the van, Bill started the engine and we threw poor Nicholas, aka Green Monster, in the back and beat a very frightened retreat.

We were driven out of Kirkby with a mob of around 100 kids behind us. They didn't exactly grasp the point of the show. In fact, they hit the Green Monster with a plank of wood at one point. Afterwards in the bar, we concluded that perhaps Kirkby was not quite ready for street theatre.

The first time I met Bill Nighy was a memorable moment. Having arrived by train, he asked me carefully one lunchtime, 'Do you drink at all? Fancy a pint?' as though in fear and dread of meeting a teetotaller. It was the beginning of a lot of fun. We all went down to the pub and then started a year of the most almighty revelry and debauchery you could ever wish to have. It was a wonderful time, the best working year of my life. We worked hard and we played even harder. Every night seemed to be a hilarious search for laughter and sex, and we often found the two together. Now that was better than working in a solicitors' office. We all had unspeakable digs in Huskinson Street, where the prostitutes operated, and enjoying ourselves began in earnest.

It was a colourful neighbourhood just across from the art college which John Lennon and Paul McCartney had occasionally attended. My favourite Beatle was George Harrison, whom I was going to play later in the musical *John, Paul, George, Ringo and Bert* which Alan Dossor directed. The original casting was me as George

Harrison, Peter Postlethwaite as John Lennon, Trevor Eve as Paul McCartney and Tony Sher as Ringo Starr. It didn't happen because Postlethwaite and I were doing something else, so Bernard Hill played Lennon and Philip Joseph played George Harrison instead of me. The prospect of playing your heroes was breathtaking. I was very disappointed when I couldn't do it.

Liverpool was a hard but entertaining city with a vibrant life and character you could almost reach out and touch. I was in 20 Huskisson Street in a flat owned by Alan Evans who used to manage The Beatles. We were always bunking down at each other's places, but we spent most of our time in clubs and chasing after women. On a typical day, we used to finish the play at half ten. The bar in the theatre would be open until 11. Then there was this other bar you could drink in until 12 o'clock. — When that closed we'd go to a club that was just down the road. After our first week at The Everyman, we went to the club called Chauffeur's for the first time, me, Bill Nighy, Nicholas le Prevost and our growing gang of good-time boys.

We used to say to any club owners or bouncers who would listen, 'How about us getting in free if we bring people down from the theatre?' Frequently, they fell for it. So they worked out a deal where four or five of us got in free every night, as long as we advertised it in the theatre and brought people down after the show, which we did. We went there every night until two or three in the morning. From there, we'd go to another club, The Somali, on Upper Parliament Street. It was always lively — it had apparently seen several murders, stabbings, and had even had a bomb thrown into it. The Somali was a real vice-den, but you could drink until five or six in the morning in relative safety. Many of the Liverpool prostitutes used to end up there, and we'd often have intriguing chats with them. After all that, we would collapse into the nearest or most inviting bed and turn in for rehearsals at 10.00am the next morning looking pretty dreadful.

We all had a ball. I was a typical young man on the loose. The young ladies of Liverpool were absolutely bloody brilliant. Young actors Nick le Prevost, Nick Stringer and Matthew Kelly joined in and every night was club night. It wasn't just one night — we never stopped. Liverpool always had this wonderful atmosphere.

But there was some real acting as well. Jonathan Pryce is a lovely fellow but he was very ambitious. Even then he knew where he was going. When we did *The Taming of the Shrew* with a chap called Del Henney, Del was Petruchio and Jonathan Pryce's girlfriend (and now wife) Kate Fahy was Kate. I was Grumio, but Del and Kate didn't get on at all. The next play was a four-hander called *The Sea Anchor* by Ted Whitehead. It was what made me, and what eventually got me to the Royal Court in London. Del Henney, Stephanie Fayerman, Kate Fahy and I were supposed to be doing it. Then Jonathan asked to meet Del one Sunday lunchtime after we had finished *The Taming of the Shrew* to talk to him about the play, I was with him at the Philharmonic pub beforehand, but I eventually left so they could talk. The conversation was somewhat one-sided, as Jonathan Pryce sacked Del Henney amid much acrimony and bad feeling.

It was very hard on Del who is a fine actor, but it was how future Oscar nominee Pete Postlethwaite joined the company. On my first meeting with the wild man of acting, I realised Pete was a powerful lover of life who would definitely not be a man to get on the wrong side of. Fortunately, we got on like a house on fire straight away. I always remember having a game of darts with him and realising he was so competitive at everything, he just had to win the game. We were very close but there was always this competitive edge to him, and I remember him once saying, 'This bloke worries me — he's too bloody good,' and being immensely flattered to learn that he was talking about me. Postlethwaite was then enjoying a stormy and passionate relationship with an unknown but very talented young actress called Julie Walters.

Del was rightly very upset to be sacked. He was a good actor and it showed me that Jonathan was pretty ruthless. It worked well because Postlethwaite was such an amazing actor. I have worked with some great actors but I'd rate him as the best. It was a hard decision for Jonathan to make. Del was very angry and I'm not sure he ever really recovered from it. But Pos was so good that he helped the play to work brilliantly, and it was through my performance in it that a casting director called Patsy Pollock from the Royal Court eventually asked me to visit her. She said she would be in touch, and I thought I'd never hear from her again. But she did get in touch, and that was what eventually brought me to London.

Pos and I were drunk a lot of the time. We drank pints and pints of beer together — we couldn't afford anything stronger as we were only on £26 a week. And we used to do pub theatre with Scully, the character that launched Alan Bleasdale's reputation. Postlethwaite was Scully, Matthew Kelly was Mooey, I was Snotty Dog and Julie Walters was Mrs Scully.

We used to have some wild times. Liverpool pubs are

hard, and we had to have minders with us for safety. One night, Postlethwaite was on doing his Scully bit and we hadn't come on yet, but one member of the audience was a few drinks ahead of the rest of the planet. He was shouting, 'Where's that f****** c**t Snotty Dog? I'm going to kick his f***** head in.'

I was waiting in the wings and Postlethwaite, who can be relied upon to handle anything, coolly said to this bloke, 'It's OK, mate, he's coming on in a minute — you can have a chat with him.' I was terrified. Matthew was on next and I was after him and there was this mad drunk out there who wanted to kill me. In the end he was led out — there was a scuffle and he tried to get on stage to get me. I didn't know what I'd done — he didn't know me, Kevin Lloyd, he just hated Snotty Dog. Luckily, Postlethwaite was very strong (he trained as a PE teacher, so he was a good bloke to have around), and he is still very fit.

Brecht's *Coriolanus* was another highlight. Geoffrey Reeves from the Nottingham Playhouse directed it. Postlethwaite was Coriolanus and he was brilliant. I was Brutus; Bill Nighy was Tullus Afidius; Nick le Prevost was Menenius; Matthew Kelly was in there somewhere and so was Julie Walters. But it's Geoffrey Durham I remember most clearly as the Leader of the Senate.

It was such a successful production that we were packed every night at the Everyman. And naturally because it was a very heavy play there was an awful lot of giggling going on. Nick le Prevost, Nick Stringer (who was playing the other tribune, Sicinius) and I just couldn't look at each other because, after every scene, we would be left together plotting and we kept breaking up with laughter. One night, just before the final scene where Coriolanus is sentenced to death in front of the

Senate, we were all on stage and Geoff Durham had to deliver a dramatic speech passing the sentence of death. This unfortunately involved a very complicated quick change. There is not a lot of room in the wings at the Everyman so it was rather cramped. Poor Geoff suffers from bad eyesight and he had not noticed after his change that he still had a wire coat-hanger stuck in his toga. As the lights went up for this supreme dramatic moment, there was just no hiding it. It was there and we were all fighting the laughter. The audience soon realised and they started laughing. In the end, everyone but Geoff knew what we were all laughing about and the high drama was sadly lost that night. Afterwards, Geoff said, 'What was wrong?' We had to tell him, and he was mortified.

Laughter was very much the order of the day on stage in Liverpool. In Willy Russell's *Breezeblock Park* the usual crew was joined by an actor called Christopher Blake, then much in demand for commercials. Director Alan Dossor had instructed that in one scene the television was supposed to be on and, as it was switched to ITV, the adverts came on. Of course, Christopher Blake soon appeared on the telly and Postlethwaite decided to depart from the script. He looked at the screen and announced, 'He's good. He's very good.' We all killed ourselves at that on stage, but I'm not at all sure the audience got the joke.

Getting involved in scrapes involving women seemed to be very much the order of the day. I can well recall my most embarrassing moment which still gives me a nervous shudder. We used to have different girls all the time, never really going home. I remember going out with a young lady whom Bill Nighy had gone out with previously. We were very good mates and we used to share girlfriends sometimes.

We were rehearsing *Funny Peculiar*. The woman in question was separated from her husband, and I had gone back to her house and stayed the night before the next morning's rehearsals at 10.00am. Unfortunately, at 9.00am the front door burst open and it was her husband. I later learned that he was the son of a famous comedy writer. He'd come round to talk to his wife about the kids, but she obviously didn't want him to know that I was there, so she locked me in the bedroom while she went down to talk to him.

But he never left. They just sat there talking and the conversation went on for ages. I started to panic because I was due at rehearsals and there I was, locked in this woman's bedroom. In the end, I shinned down the drainpipe which I was horrified to discover took me straight past the window where they were talking. But my luck was in — he had his back to me. They were talking about the kids. I remember seeing her eyes widen as she tried to keep the look of surprise off her face, and I certainly didn't hang around. I ran all the way to Hope Street. I was an hour-and-a-half-late and Alan Dossor was, quite rightly, absolutely furious.

Being at the Everyman at that time was magical. The three writers at the Everyman were brilliant: Willy Russell, Alan Bleasdale and Mike Stott. Yet no one had ever heard of them. It's amazing to think of the talent they had and none of them were known.

When we first moved to Liverpool, we all lived in Dossor's house which was domestically unorthodox. That was quite an experience. I was very naïve. I'd been to drama school so I knew people didn't always live in conventional family units, but Alan had turned his house into a commune, although he didn't seem to be there a lot of the time. His wife, Di, is a lovely lady, and they had a daughter called Lucy. But Di was living there together with another bloke called Terry, along with Dossor and everyone else who had arrived in Liverpool.

Alan was very kind and very relaxed. On my first night there, I even had to share a bed with a bloke, but nothing happened. The whole of the Everyman was run like a commune — I think that is at least partly why it was so bloody great. We spent 24 hours a day with each other. I think the only time we were apart was late at night if we'd managed to pull a bird. I have this image in my mind of Di in bed with Terry and Alan kneeling at the side of the bed, saying, 'Where did it all go wrong?' It was like living in a madhouse, but then it was also a fascinating introduction to theatrical life.

Matthew Kelly has gone from strength to strength since I first met him as just another unknown struggling actor keen to make his name. He was married with two kids when I knew him and he was a lovely fellow. I used to babysit for him. Matthew was brilliant at playing gormless parts. In *Funny Peculiar* he was a mentally retarded character with a hole in his head and he was fantastic, very, very funny. He had to be given the right part. You couldn't really ask him to play Romeo looking like he does. And he never ventured out womanising and drinking. He was married and he went home, and when he couldn't, he stayed with me. There was no hint of the quizmaster then.

The lads in the company used to get into quite a few fights. We were a butch outfit. Postlethwaite could look after himself, I used to do a bit of boxing and Bill Nighy and Nick le Prevost could handle themselves if necessary. The locals used to come round to the theatre for a late drink and there was always a little bit of friction between them and us 'poofy' actors. There was one scrap which started when a drunken Scouser had poured loud and foul-mouthed scorn on our masculinity.

We said one or two things back and suddenly all hell was let loose. I can remember Alan Dossor, whose remark had started it all, doing one of those prudent dives and going out through everyone's legs. He left us lot to be smashed to pulp. It finally drew to an exhausted and bloody close and we declared it an honourable draw, mercifully just before the police arrived.

It was a dangerous theatre. You couldn't get much more edge than Jonathan Pryce and Pete Postlethwaite. I didn't do badly in the competition to attract as many girls as possible because, believe it or not, I wasn't bad looking then. But Bill Nighy used to have them absolutely swooning over him. They all thought he looked like James Dean. He really would have preferred to be a pop singer and he loved dancing. We used to take the mickey because he preferred to sing rather than act. But most of the time he was on the phone trying to sort out his deeply complicated love-life. He was always talking to girls he had left behind. There just weren't enough hours in the day for Bill to fit them all in.

We competed for women. I remember him stopping me one night at a club when we met up with an older woman I had gone off with two or three nights earlier. She really was quite a lot older. Bill approached and said, somewhat ungallantly, 'Look surely you're not going to go off with her again. She is just too rough.' He tried to stop me, without any success. Postlethwaite got together with Julie early on and they had three or four very close years together. Julie packed up her boyfriend and moved in with Postlethwaite, who behaved himself probably better than any of us, at that level anyway.

We had loads of all-night parties and very often we used to turn up for rehearsals not having been to bed. If you're dancing all night long you can drink a lot of alcohol and I don't think any of us ate. Eating didn't come into it. They used to throw us scraps at Chauffeur's — usually some left over chicken and chips. We must have gone down in history there because we brought them a lot of trade. The real diehards were Postlethwaite, Bill and me, and when Chauffeur's shut at three we used to go on to a club which was really rough — murders used to happen there, people got stabbed and once a bomb was thrown in. It was a complete vice den but you could drink until five or six o'clock in the morning in perfect safety. All the Liverpool prostitutes came in there later on. We'd often have an enlightening chat. It was a very educational time of my life; I learned a lot about looking after myself, and about women.

Nick Stringer, who was later to appear in *Coronation Street* as well as *The Bill*, was the sensible one among us. He used to lecture me all the time. He would say, 'You've got to settle down and stop all this boozing and chasing after different women.' And I used to say, 'Yeah, yeah, yeah,' and pay no attention to him at all. While all the rest of us went out on the town, he and Matthew Kelly were the only ones who used to rush off home.

Nick went back to his girlfriend, Cheryl, and eventually they were married, but, after all those years of toeing the line and good behaviour, the marriage lasted about three months. I still joke with him about it. He really might as well have come out with us and enjoyed himself.

The houses we lived in were bloody terrible. I rented a room on the top floor in Huskinson Street. There was an art student in the next room and some other people from the theatre living there as well. One night, having taken an older woman back home, she got up to go to the toilet and, of course, she wandered back into the wrong room and got into bed with the art student. There was a terrible scream from my neighbour who was horrified at being woken up by a woman old enough to be his mother climbing into bed with him and starting to cuddle him. He had a real go at me the next day. I was surprised. Some blokes would have thanked me.

Another night, I was all on my own in bed at 4.00am when suddenly the lights went on and we were all woken by an ear-splitting scream. It was Alethia, the stage manager from the theatre. She used to sleep on a mattress on the floor in her ground-floor flat. Whilst she was sleeping, she had felt something pressing on her chest and opened her eyes to see a large rat staring at her. She was in a terrible state. We had to call in a doctor for her. The health authority was also called, and the house was closed down the next day. But Alethia underwent treatment for ages.

They were great days because, back in Derby, my heroes Brian Clough and Peter Taylor were turning my team into the best side in the land, and I used to make regular pilgrimages back to the Baseball Ground. My mum always sent me the green football special. Kevin Hector, Colin Todd, John O'Hare and Roy McFarland were my heroes, and Cloughie was God.

I loved my time in Liverpool but my departure was a little unfortunate. I had been in seven marvellous plays, including the first production of Willy Russell's *Breezeblock Park* and Brecht's *Coriolanus, The Pig and the*

Junkle, and *The Sea Anchor*. I was in the original version of *Funny Peculiar* which went on to win Comedy of the Year, and ran for four years at the Garrick Theatre in London. I played Desmond Ainsley, a wonderful part.

There's an amazing bun-fight in the play that goes on for 20 minutes. Julie Walters' character had just found out that her husband had been having an affair. They run the local bakery. I was Desmond, the lunatic local delivery man who comes in whistling 'Lipstick on your collar told a tale or two'. He's one of those idiots who cracks jokes all the time. The husband, Trevor, played by Nick le Prevost, asks for his order of two dozen cream puffs. Desmond comes back in with the real thing, supplied every night by the local bakery, and sets them out along the counter. Then he just goes berserk and smashes them all up. Cream went everywhere. Sometimes we could hardly do it for laughing. We then switch to fighting with washing-up liquid. Then I run out to the van for more ammunition. A bubble-gum machine breaks in the course of the fight. Dossor staged it brilliantly. It is the funniest scene I've ever come across. The climax is a pie in each face. All the blinds went down and I then put my hand through the door in a final act of defiance and for some reason that brought the house down. It's wonderful when things come to you as you're working, and that was one of them. We won the Best Comedy award with it.

In the end, Postlethwaite had to play that part in the West End because I was already there in another play. Patsy Pollock from the Royal Court came and asked me if I would be interested in joining them. She wanted me to meet Albert Finney because they were doing a Joe Orton season — *Loot, Entertaining Mr Sloane* and *What the Butler Saw*. Finney was directing *Loot*, Lindsay

Anderson was directing *What the Butler Saw* and Roger Croucher was doing *Entertaining Mr Sloane*. They had got Malcolm McDowell, Beryl Reid and Ronald Fraser for Mr Sloane, and Albert was casting *Loot*. He had already cast Jill Bennett, and he was still looking for the two boys.

CHAPTER FOUR

THE BIG BREAK

So I was going to see Albert Finney. It was 1975 and the fat lad from Derby who used to work in a solicitors' office was going to London to talk about acting on stage. In London. With Albert Finney. I had to pinch myself. But then, tragedy. I got a phonecall from Finney just before I caught the train, saying that he was sorry but he had already cast the play. He had lined up David Troughton and James Aubrey as the two lads, and, naturally, I felt very disappointed. All my hopes of stardom were dashed. I thought I had missed out there.

But then I got another phonecall and my hopes soared again. I was asked to come to see Lindsay Anderson who was casting *What the Butler Saw*. It can be a heart-stopping business acting, from despair to delight in the space of a moment, and back again, of course. But this time the part was a genuine gem. Even I could see that. In all of Joe Orton's tremendously wild and anarchic plays, the author always drew one character very close to himself. In *What the Butler Saw* it's Nicholas Beckett, the role I was to be considered for.

When I first came down to see Patsy Pollock, Lindsay Anderson had walked into the office we were in. He had seen me and said 'Hello'. Apparently, he had been looking everywhere for someone to play Nicholas Beckett and had mentioned me to Patsy. He'd said, 'Who's that boy? Can he come down and audition.' Can he? I'd have crawled down the M6 if necessary. It seems crazy that a chance meeting like that can change your life.

There was a big picture of Joe Orton outside the theatre when I arrived and even I thought he didn't look unlike me in those days. I had a long audition with Lindsay at the Royal Court. You get this feeling as an actor about auditions. Nobody really likes them as a rule but, just occasionally, when they go well they can be enjoyable. I knew it was going well but then I started to feel nervous. This was a chance of a big London break, the possibility of a big part at the Joe Orton Festival and I'd had a good start. Could I really carry it off?

I knew I was near to clinching it. The audition ended and Lindsay Anderson just said he would be in touch. I didn't know what that meant, and when I got back to the Liverpool Everyman I found that Dossor had posted the cast list for the new play *Under New Management* by Chris Bond, and I had been given the leading part. I wasn't actually under contract, but I did have a certain understanding with the Everyman. Then I received another phonecall the next day from Patsy Pollock to tell me that Lindsay Anderson thought he wanted me for the part. But he still had to cast the girl, which did have a bearing on my casting because they turn out to be twins. And until he had cast the girl who was going to be my twin, he couldn't make a final decision. In the meantime, could I leave myself open?

I said I had just been offered the main part in a new production, and Patsy said 'Couldn't you stall them?' I couldn't really. Dossor already knew that I'd been to the Royal Court and was unhappy about it. I heard nothing so I did the first two days of rehearsals of *Under New Management* and, of course, a telegram then arrived from the Royal Court making the official offer. Jane Carr had been cast as my sister and, fortunately, we did look quite alike. Betty Marsden, Valentine Dyall, Michael Medwin and Brian Glover made up the rest of the cast.

I just didn't know what to do. I went to Alan Dossor and showed him the telegram. He went berserk, but just as he was hitting the roof the telephone rang. It was Patsy Pollock from the Royal Court saying, 'Look, can you do us a favour, can you let Kevin out? You've only just started rehearsing.' He agreed, but it wasn't exactly gracious. He smashed the phone down and said with feeling, 'F*** off.'

We're mates now I am very happy to say, and I can quite understand his anger at being let down by an ambitious and seemingly ungrateful young actor. He was totally unimpressed by the glitter of the Royal Court. We both had a point, but I was in a terrible position. He threw me out of rehearsals saying, 'F*** off and do your trendy stuff down in London.' My situation was made worse by the fact that I was also playing Tommy in *Breezeblock Park* at the time, a wonderful part and I was getting rave reviews for it.

Julie Walters was my wife, and I still had four weeks of that to run. Alan Dossor didn't speak to me again until long after I had left.

I had been in Liverpool for just over a year. I knew with a frightening clarity that this was my big break. Lindsay Anderson was a name to conjure with. He was right at the peak of his fame then, and the great Albert Finney was associated as well. This was exalted company indeed. It was the big time and I realised that I wanted it. I wanted it very much. It meant leaving the cosy and alarmingly sociable world of lovely Liverpool and all my mates. Dossor called in Pip Donaghy at short notice to take over from me in *Under New Management*. I left under a bit of a cloud, but mates like Postlethwaite and Bill Nighy told me I simply had to go for it. In fact, Bill had auditioned for the same part as me and I thought he'd get it because he's better looking. It did upset me, moving on. I was leaving my mates and I liked and respected Dossor very much and didn't want to fall out with him. He brought out some of my best stage work. But I knew there was only one choice to make.

It was the summer of 1975 when I boarded another train to London to begin a new chapter in my life. As a leaving present, Postlethwaite gave me a 1946 Derby County FA Cup Winner's medal, which was a pretty special gift as far as I was concerned. I never did find out exactly how he got that. We all went out for a meal on my last night and he presented me with it. It knocked me out. Pos had been sharing a flat in London which he didn't need any more, so I moved in with a couple of acting brothers called Brian and Eric Deacon. Brian Deacon was going out with a completely unknown actress called Rula Lenska at the time, so she was around quite a bit and they eventually got married. I arrived with my single case, like Charlie Chaplin in *The Tramp*, completely ignorant of central London and everyone in it. The flat was in elegant Harrington Gardens in deepest South Kensington. I didn't even realise that I had landed a highly fashionable address. I just got off the train and looked at the Tube map and found it. I'd never even met my two flatmates before. Brian wasn't there that much. Strangely, he seemed to prefer Rula's company to mine. Funny that!

In fact, I was with Rula when she got her big break in *Rock Follies*, the drama series about an all-girl pop group. She was terribly nervous about going for the interview because she couldn't sing, which was a bit of a drawback for a role as a pop star. But she got it. We went and had a drink in one of the pubs in South Kensington before she went off for the audition. She was a lovely, very striking girl. I thought that if the women look like that here, maybe South Kensington isn't such a bad place to live.

But I went out and had a drink alone, feeling very lonely the night before I started rehearsals. I was scared to death not knowing my flatmates or the future cast, but realising how important this chance was for me. I knew it could change my life.

It took just about all the bottle I had to turn up for the first readthrough. I remember the sweat dripping off me because of my nerves. Alan Price from *The Animals* wrote the music so he was there. All those famous faces were dazzling, and there was little me. Socialising with people like Malcolm McDowell was pretty amazing for a young lad from Derby. Lindsay Anderson was very kind to me. He could see I was in danger of being overwhelmed and he took me under his wing, introducing me to everyone. He helped me to fit into the Royal Court. I had gone a long way upmarket from the deliciously down-to-earth world of the Liverpool Everyman. All of a sudden, I was treading the same boards as Laurence Olivier, John Gielgud, Alan Bates and Albert Finney.

I achieved fame rather than riches. I was on £56 a week. In the nicest possible way I had been somewhat stitched up. They had me sign a contract stating that if it transferred to the West End, as they hoped it would, then my pay would go up to the princely sum of £65 a week. In those days, £65 seemed a lot of money, but for a starring role in the West End it was peanuts. There were only six of us in the play and I had my name up in huge lights. Brian Glover, who is very worldly wise and quickly became a close friend and adviser, said quietly one night, 'They did you up a bit, didn't they?' I was young and naïve and so keen to play the part I'd have signed anything and they knew it.

One morning before we opened, I had to meet Lindsay Anderson and Jocelyn Herbert, the designer, at 9.00 am outside Selfridges, to kit me out with my costume. That was quite an experience. Lindsay led us to the wig department and asked to look 'at the auburn range, for this gentleman here', meaning me. The assistant almost fainted, as everyone else in sight was female. It was highly embarrassing and it got worse. After the wigs, we went across the road to find a pair of high-heeled shoes for me to learn to walk in them instantly. I had to try on a lot of different pairs before I found some that I could stay upright in, let alone walk. The assistants must have thought we were crazy. Then I got the leopard-skin dress. 'Thank goodness my mum isn't here,' was all that kept running through my mind.

We rehearsed in a church hall in Paddington. Nicholas Beckett plays a page-boy who's into everything. He's more AC/DC than high-voltage electricity and he ends up dressing as a woman. Although I say it myself, I've not got bad legs, and in my red wig and leopard-skin dress I looked quite something. When I played the part, I got loads of fan-mail from homosexuals, which was something else that opened my eyes. The gay people loved it, and the nightly queues for return tickets seemed to get longer and longer.

Orton was their king and I was playing him, so I suppose it was no surprise that I became the centre of attention. I had to streak across the stage in one scene — that was the most embarrassing thing I've had to do in my life. Jane Carr had to get down to her bra and pants which she was a bit worried about. But I had to take everything off. After about three weeks of rehearsals, Lindsay said quietly one morning: 'I think we'll have to do it for real today,' and my heart sank. I did it and then of course he stopped the scene to talk about it and I was left there, stark-bollock-naked, not knowing where to put my hands. And everyone else had got clothes on. They were all being terribly polite and looking me straight in the eye, trying not to look anywhere else. It was awful that first time but, funnily enough, it was perfectly all right afterwards. We didn't have to talk about it anymore. I just did it.

I had three changes of clothes. I had to dress up as a copper in the play as well. I was changing out of my copper's uniform once, and Lindsay got the idea for the publicity photo from that famous photograph of the policeman covering a football streaker with his helmet. As I ran across the stage, Betty Marsden came out of the opposite door and saw me like that. It was just a streak but it brought the house down. And after that first time, doing it every night wasn't a problem. There was even a bit of a fight among the dressers as to who was going to help me to take my underpants off, but that's another story.

The show was a success right from the beginning, and we soon transferred to the Whitehall Theatre. Soon afterwards, I was nominated as Best Newcomer. It was an amazing time for me. On the opening night, I could have died and gone to heaven happy. I shared a dressing-room with Brian Glover and I just remember being absolutely speechless with nerves. I said to Brian, 'Don't you get nervous?' and he said 'No, no,' but I knew he meant 'Yes'. I was so shocked by Brian's tragically early death. It was such a sad loss to our business. Then there was a knock on the door and it was Albert Finney wanting to wish us all the best. I couldn't believe it. Albert Finney, my hero, *Saturday Night and Sunday Morning*, *Tom Jones* and all that. Wishing *me* good luck. Because I was a Northern lad, he seemed to really like me. He told me how he did press-ups before he went on stage to relax himself. I got on with him like a house on fire. All the major critics were filing in and I'm there in my dressing-room with Albert Finney. That almost made me feel worse. Then the door opened again and Sir John Gielgud was there, saying, 'All the best. I hope your London début is the first of many.' He even brought some flowers for me.

I was going by this time, I'd just about reached climax point. Glover was saying, 'Don't worry lad ... be all right ... nothing to worry about,' then with ten minutes to go, the door opens again and in walks Sir Ralph Richardson. I was just about on the floor at this point. There I am, on the biggest night of my life, and all my acting heroes were wishing *me* good luck. It took some getting used to. He had starred in the original version of the play. I just couldn't believe I was suddenly moving in such exalted company. The only person who wasn't there was Olivier, who was ill at the time. Alan Bates was somewhere in the building and yet I was the one getting all the attention!

'Crikey!' I thought, 'I wish my dad could see me now.' I made a bolt for the loo because my nerves had taken a turn for the worse and then the five-minute call came over the tannoy. I remember thinking, 'I really want to be home, waiting for my mates to come round to take me to the pub, like they used to do in the good old days when there was no pressure on me.' And knowing I was five minutes from going on in front of all my heroes, I was absolutely terrified.

Luckily I wasn't on until 15 minutes into the show. Michael Medwin hadn't been on stage for a long time and he was a bit worried too. You forget other people are just as nervous as you. He fluffed a few lines and I know it sounds cruel, but that made me feel better. It dawned on me that I wasn't the only one who was feeling anxious. Even Betty Marsden fluffed a line. Somehow, that gave me even greater confidence. I thought to myself, 'If they're nervous, they're just the same as me, so I can't be any worse.' Funnily enough, as I walked out on to the stage all my nerves went, and I was just left with this great feeling of excitement as I just went on and did it.

The show was a great success for me. The performance swept by in a blur. Lindsay Anderson came up to me afterwards and asked me to come out of the dressing-room and I thought I was going to get a bollocking for something. He just said quietly, 'I want to

tell you that that is the best London début I've ever
seen.' Which was praise indeed from him. And he gave
me a first-night present of a book, a copy of *This Sporting
Life* by David Storey, which Lindsay had made into a
film starring Richard Harris. In it, he borrowed a phrase
from the book. He wrote 'You played a blinder.' And the
reviews were great; the critics said that I had got the
style right. It was the talk of London for a while. Coming
to the Royal Court to see *What the Butler Saw* was very
trendy.

Lindsay was wonderful. He saw something in me and
became, in a way, my guiding light in the business. I
went to work for him again in the film *Britannia Hospital*
in 1983, and in a marvellous production of *The Playboy of
the Western World*. Wherever I worked after that, he
always kept in touch with me and was always at the end
of a telephone or sent a letter with words of sound
advice. If I had any problems in my career, I would turn
to him. He was absolutely marvellous. He was my
mentor.

Then we moved to the Whitehall. We had opened in
August at the Royal Court and did eight weeks there,
and then opened at the Whitehall in September. I was on
such a high I couldn't do anything wrong. I was invited
to parties and given free membership of big clubs.
Suddenly, I had to smarten up my act a little. My mates
came down to visit and it was great to see them. And
that is when I met Lesley.

My mum never really believed me when I told her I
had my name up in lights a yard high in the West End —
until she came down and saw it for herself. She was very
worried about me being in London because, not only
were all actors raving poofs, but the city was full of
drugs and prostitutes and all sorts of disgusting things.

When I met her off the train at St Pancras, she was certainly on her guard. The area was full of posters which included some of me, naked apart from a policeman's helmet covering my doings. It was all over the back of hundreds of buses.

We got on a bus to go back to my flat. I had been up early that morning to make it look presentable. Sitting at the front on the top deck, Mum was still in full flow, warning me about the dangers of living in London. Then we suddenly came right up behind another bus on which was the poster of me — naked. My mother didn't recognise me and said, 'Look, that's what goes on down here, that's the sort of thing I'm worried about.'

I had to say to her, as gently as I could manage, 'Mum, that's me.' She had no idea. When she came to see *What the Butler Saw*, which must be one of the rudest plays I've ever come across, if not the rudest, I really was fearing the worst. Fortunately, my mother never understood a word. Necrophilia wasn't a word that registered with her; I was delighted to learn that it simply was not in her vocabulary. And all these racy lines like 'Bury her in a Y shaped coffin' went mercifully way over her head. I was dreading her reaction but, in fact, she astonished me by saying she thought it was rather good. She just couldn't understand why I had to strip off in it. She thought that was a little unnecessary, but apart from that she quite liked the play.

I didn't have a woman in my life at all around this time. I had left one relationship behind in Liverpool and I was thoroughly enjoying my independence. I was the furthest away from settling down that I had ever been. I was enjoying life so much I didn't want a proper, permanent relationship. It was such a great time, everyone seemed to want to know me. Michael Medwin had a friend, a successful antique dealer, who invited me to a party. I'd met him in Michael's dressing room. I was going out with Michael's girlfriend's daughter very briefly. He said, 'You can't refuse, he is a millionaire, you must go.'

But this antique dealer also turned out to be extremely gay, and he firmly instructed Michael that I was to come but I was not to bring my girlfriend. I didn't know this at the time. I just kept getting telephone messages at the theatre from this bloke asking me to ring him back. He was literally pleading with me to come to the party. I still hadn't got a clue why. That's how innocent and naïve I was. In the end, I said 'Yes'. I just became fed-up with saying 'No'.

Medwin burst into hysterical laughter when he found out how keen this bloke was to see me and put me out of my misery, 'He's a raving poof,' he explained sensitively, 'and he fancies the pants off you.' I was terrified and very shocked. But Medwin started winding me up saying, 'You've got to go,' so I got Brian Glover to go with me. And he did because we had become good friends. The antique dealer didn't mind that because Brian was another bloke. I remember saying to Brian as we arrived at his huge mansion in London, 'Just don't leave me,' and Brian promised to stand back-to-back with me all night. Brian's a lad-and-a-half but, of course, as soon as I got there, the host latched on to me and wanted to show me the house. He seemed particularly anxious to show me his bedrooms. Thank God Glover was there as my minder. It was a big society party — I remember seeing Jilly Cooper there, and I had a long chat with her, but I spent most of my time avoiding the antique dealer. He was very persistent but, mercifully, he did get the message after a while.

When I was nominated as Best Newcomer, I had called in for a social chat with Patsy Pollock when she rang up another casting agent, Mary Selway, who had liked me in the play. Patsy asked, 'What about this film you're doing, *Trial by Combat*, with John Mills? I've got Kevin here. Isn't there a part for him?' I didn't even have to audition, I simply landed the part of Little Willie in a feature. Money started to roll into my pocket for the first time. Although I still believe I was stitched up, £65 in 1975 went quite a long way and I was on my own. I think the flat cost me £12 a week, so I had the rest to spend on having a good time.

CHAPTER FIVE

LESLEY

An actor friend called Bill Rourke introduced me to the woman who was to change my life in more ways than one. Bill liked a drink, and without wishing to be too unkind, he was always a much better bar-room entertainer than he was an actor. After the show, Brian Glover used to drop me off in South Kensington and then I would carry on enjoying the evening with Bill Rourke and usually get home around 3.00 am.

One night he remarked, 'There's a very pretty blonde bird in the No Name Wine Bar, let's go and chat her up.' I didn't like wine and Bill was always spotting attractive women, so I didn't go at first. But eventually I gave in and, sure enough, there was the very pretty blonde.

From the moment I set eyes on her, I was gone. Orchestras started playing, angels fluttered around and I was simply in heaven. People who say there's no such thing as love at first sight don't know what they are talking about. I was smitten from the second I clapped eyes on Lesley. She was shy and feminine and tough and brave and so proud of her two young children. We talked and we laughed and she seemed to like me and that was it. I never wanted to look at another woman from that night onwards. It was just so simple. I wanted Lesley.

Unfortunately, Lesley thought all actors were bullshitters and over the years I have seen plenty of examples to support her theory. She had heard all the talk of auditions and egos and so on, and had formed an opinion that actors were pretty fond of their own voices. I'm sure she wasn't wrong in many cases. When she met me, I was immediately attracted to her and the very first thing she told me was that she had been married but it was over and she had two children. She wanted to make that absolutely clear as quickly as possible.

It was quite a big thing for her, of course, but it didn't matter or make any difference to me. But first we had to get over the problem of all actors being bullshitters. I don't think I'm one of them. I'm different, I think. But when I told her I was playing a starring role in a West End play, and I wanted her to come and see it, I started to sound highly unbelievable. Of course she thought that wasn't true, that I was just like all the other actors she had met and that I was stringing her along. She said she would come, but she told me later that she didn't believe anything I had said.

In fact, I was also doing the film *Trial by Combat*, so I was really busy filming during the day and doing the stage show at night. I said I would come in the next night and sort the tickets out for her, but I was so busy I never found time to go back to the wine bar. Naturally, when I went in a few days later, she was very off with me. She thought I had been telling her a pack of lies and that I was a bullshitter like all the rest of the actors she had met. When I first asked her out, Lesley was so wary of actors that she asked a friend of hers to look me up in *Spotlight*, the actors' directory, to see if I was a real actor. All this went on behind my back before she would agree to a date. Somehow, I eventually talked her round to coming to the show, and she agreed to come with her friend. They came to the Saturday matinée at the Whitehall to see it.

I arranged to meet her afterwards in the pub opposite, just to see what she thought. Her first words to me were, 'You never told me you took all your clothes off!' and I think she was really rather shocked. Of course, when they all found out back at the wine bar that I was completely starkers on stage, there were loads of jokes about seeing the credentials before you sample the goods. But that night after the show, I went back to the wine bar and it was basically love at first sight.

I mean that seriously — all my other relationships, apart from Hilary, had been flings. I lived with a girl called Louise who was genuinely nice, but there was nothing there. I knew when I met Lesley that this was going to be very different, and it seemed to be the same for both of us. We kissed for the first time the night following her trip to the theatre, something which shocked everybody because we did it in the wine bar. Lesley is really quite shy and she had fended off loads of other blokes before I came along.

I was the lucky one. I'm not really sure why. She said I

had a lot of life about me. She said I was different. It was certainly nothing to do with being an actor with his name up in lights in the West End. I just made her laugh, but we didn't go to bed together straight away. I went off home and she went off to where she was staying with her sister in Battersea, and I arranged to meet her on the Sunday by the lions in Trafalgar Square. But there are four bloody lions and they are quite a distance apart, so we were waiting under separate lions for about half-an-hour before it dawned on me to have a look round. She thought I had dumped her and I thought she had dumped me. We were both happy and relieved when we found each other, and we went off and watched *Gone with the Wind*.

I think we both knew right from the start that we had instantly fallen in love. How many times does that happen in your life? It was very emotional, very intense. It was only 13 months after we met that our first daughter, Chloe, was born, so you can imagine just how passionate we were about each other. Our first date was on Lesley's birthday, 18 October 1975.

The second time we went out, we went to watch the film of Woodstock, and we both really enjoyed it. I was delighted that we seemed to be very much on the same wavelength. Afterwards, we went to a restaurant in the King's Road. I was very nervous and, even though I was short of cash, I ordered a steak. Somehow, it became the most important thing in the world that the date went well, which contrived to make me so awkward and all fingers and thumbs that I managed to shoot the steak right off my plate and into Lesley's lap. That was a great start. What a great impression! We both laughed and, when the bill finally came, I found that I hadn't got enough money and I had to ask Lesley to chip in. 'What a smoothy', she must have thought. But we laughed about it. It didn't seem to matter. I was so taken with her and she seemed to be with me. She was just extremely attractive and extremely feminine and a very nice woman. I loved her, it was as simple as that.

We did get it together pretty soon afterwards, but I felt so much for her I would never have jumped into bed on the first night. With other women, I often knew it was a one-night stand and if we were both grown up and wanted to do it then that's what happened. But with Lesley, that was completely different. If she hadn't wanted to as much as me, I would happily have waited, because I knew the feelings were so different from all the rest. We slept together quite early on, and within two or three weeks we were living together. I moved into her sister's place at 37B Lurline Gardens in Battersea, and I was the happiest man in London.

I packed my few things together and told my flatmates I was going. Then I left rather hurriedly taking my duvet with me. Lesley's sister lived on her own, but she had just started going out with the consultant surgeon she eventually married.

There was just something breathtaking about Lesley. She was very feminine and funny, very much a lady. She wasn't at all ashamed about having two children. Her attitude, quite rightly, was that if I was interested in her then I had to accept the children. And I had no problem with that. We were both working during the day and I used to get complimentary tickets to the theatres, so we used to go out in the afternoons to the other matinées. Then after about two weeks, we went up to Ruthin in Wales where her parents were looking after the children, so that I could be introduced to Mark and Sophie. They were two and three at the time and they were lovely kids, both bright and sparky. I took to them both on sight and, happily, they seemed to take to me.

Lesley's husband had gone walkabout and then, when he came back, she left him. I never met him and he didn't seem too concerned about maintenance. I was so much in love with Lesley that the prospect of two young children just didn't matter at all, they just all came together as a package. I have always been good with kids, so I wasn't worried. After about another two or three weeks, they came down to London to live with us there.

We all moved in together very quickly. At first, we stayed at Lesley's sister's in Battersea, and then we bought a house. I think that is what first started the resentment towards me from the in-laws, because I 'took' the children away. They were very attached to Mark and Sophie and, if I hadn't come on the scene when I did, they would probably have kept them in Wales. I know my prospective mother-in-law felt very aggrieved at that.

Lesley was very brave to have left an unhappy marriage and set out for London to try to build a new life for herself. She wasn't looking for a bloke, it just happened between us. She came to London to get a job so she could buy a flat, bring the children down and live near her sister. She wanted to break away from her bad memories and her mother. I never saw her husband, which is probably just as well. I would probably have shown him exactly how I felt about his treatment of Lesley.

Lesley had been struggling financially, and hadn't been helped by her husband's refusal to give her any support. I wasn't in a much better position myself. We received no help at all and, like a lot of actors, I was hopeless with money. I had had a little bit of success on the stage, but I had done no television. So we brought the children up on what little money we had, which certainly wasn't a fortune. *What the Butler Saw* finished in January after a six-month run, and then, typically, when I most needed a decent income, I had three months of nothing, the longest period out of work I've had. It was very frightening. I had taken on a partner with an instant family and I was suddenly desperately short of money.

So when I got the chance to audition for a musical, I jumped at it. The producers of *What the Butler Saw* thought that they'd seen something else in me. They were also producing *The Rocky Horror Show*, and they wanted me to take over as Frank-n-Furter after *What the Butler Saw* finished. That is, they did until they heard me sing. They just assumed that because I was young, slim, looked the part and had gathered critical acclaim, that I would be perfect for it. I went down to the King's Road to audition and, I have to admit, I was quite appalling. A friend had come to the house to help me practise my singing. At that time, I used to sing 'Sorrow' by the Merseybeats endlessly to try to improve. In fact, I used to sing two other songs as well, but, unfortunately, all three sounded exactly the same. When I was up in the top room trying to master the songs, I would sometimes hear giggling outside. I'd whip open the door to find Lesley and the kids having hysterics outside. There would be shouts of 'Pathetic!' which was pretty generous. I can't keep time or hold a note. As a singer I am hopeless, and the audition for *The Rocky Horror Show* was deeply embarrassing. They were horrified. Eventually, they uttered the immortal lines, 'We'll let you know.' But I think I already knew. I remember walking home over Battersea Bridge, thinking, 'This is the most embarrassing day of my life.' That must have been one of the worst auditions I have ever done. Needless to say, I didn't get the part.

Money was very short and I even took a job in Scotland for two weeks. This was when I first realised what Lesley was made of. She is a real worker. She never stopped. As well as looking after the children, she was cooking food for solicitors in London. That was good fun. You can still have a laugh when you're skint. She had this contract providing food for some posh solicitors in South Molton Street. We would take the kids to school in the morning, go and get the greengroceries and come back to prepare the meals. I would come with her, drop it all off and pick everything up afterwards, and we always had a laugh working together.

We left Lesley's sister's in Battersea when we bought our own maisonette nearby, and we stayed there for 12 years. Lesley became pregnant very quickly. We met in October 1975 and she had Chloe on 4 November 1976. It was very fast but it was what we both wanted. Chloe was very much wanted. Our relationship was rock-solid right from the start.

Once we had our own child, getting married seemed to be the responsible thing to do. I wanted to do it. I thought it would be forever. We got married not because we had to, but to celebrate our love for each other. I proposed properly, taking Lesley out for a meal. And I even went and asked her father's permission, even though we had been living together for a while. I was terrified about having to do that. We were on a family day out to Cobham in Surrey. It was a lovely, sunny day and I was quite determined to do things the correct way, even then.

I psyched myself up for the big question and then came out with, 'I would like to ask you for your daughter's hand in marriage,' and he got all formal and embarrassed. He said, 'Er well, yes,' and everything was fine. It meant a lot to me to do things correctly. We had also started the necessary proceedings for me to adopt Mark and Sophie legally, but the formalities hadn't yet been completed.

It was made more difficult because Lesley's first husband simply refused to answer any of the solicitor's letters. We managed to sort things out eventually. I thought I got on well with her parents at first and for a long time into our marriage. My mother-in-law was always a bit unpredictable, not just for me but for everybody. I took Mark and Sophie on when they were two and three and eventually adopted them. I've never talked about it publicly before because I never wanted there to be any difference between them and the children Lesley and I had together. They are all the same to me, all our children.

We were married the following spring, on 26 March 1977 at Wandsworth Town Hall, and we had a blessing at St Mary's Church on the Thames afterwards. The witnesses were my brother, Terry, who is a journalist, and Lesley's sister, Denise, and my mum and Lesley's mum. It was quite funny because the registrar kept calling me Lloyd as if it was my first name all the way through the ceremony. And I hadn't been to a wedding for quite some time so I wasn't that sure of the procedure. I thought that maybe the laws had changed, and now they called the bloke by his surname all the way through. He kept saying, 'Do you, Lloyd, take Lesley to be your lawful wedded wife?' I thought, 'Cheeky sod! But maybe that's how they do it.' I didn't know. I hadn't been through it before. And I kept on wondering until he came to the end and said, 'Oh, I'm terribly sorry, it's Kevin, isn't it?' So I'm not really sure if we're married to this day!

Throughout the ceremony, this lovely old bloke kept opening the door and interrupting to ask, 'Is Prescott on yet?' and we kept having to tell him, 'Not yet. No, no, it's still Lloyd. Would you mind getting out?' In the end, when he came in for the umpteenth time, I felt like turning round and yelling at him, 'Will you get out. This is *my* wedding!' We had everybody back to our house. My parents-in-law came. They were right behind it. The problem was that my mother-in-law wanted to help in every aspect of the wedding, which was stressful. But we had no money and my father-in-law bore the costs. We didn't have a honeymoon — we couldn't afford one — and I was working at the time anyway. Our honeymoon came a year later when we went off to St Ives on our first holiday. I never minded, because I was so happy.

We were gloriously happy even though we had no money. I was always working but the pay was often very low. I auditioned for the esteemed Bristol Old Vic and having had three months out of work, I was in heaven when I heard that I had got in. I was with the theatre director Richard Cotterill, his assistant Michael Joyce, and this young, wheezy, asthmatic chap called Adrian Noble. He had just left university and this was his first directing job.

Although I was starring at the Bristol Old Vic, I remember my pay was £56.50 and I was the lead. They made me a pair of boots to play Blunchly, the lead in *Arms and the Man* by George Bernard Shaw, and they cost £65, more than my week's wages. It's just a good job that I didn't have to pay for them. I was working away from home a lot at the time. I was doing my apprenticeship, as I called it, with the Old Vic, swapping lead parts with Alan Rickman. We were chosen to star in *Ubu Roi*, directed by Adrian Noble, one of the first plays the future head of the Royal Shakespeare Company ever professionally directed. Then we did a very famous Brecht play together called *Man Is Man*. Even then, I could see I was in exceptional company. Rickman and Noble were both, in their very different ways, very talented young men and I had to stretch myself to keep up which was very, very good for me at the time.

Adrian is younger than me, so he must have been about 25 at the time, and I was incredibly impressed when he was bold enough to try to cast Alan Bates in his production of *Titus Andronicus*. Alan was all set to do it but had to pull out (Simon Callow played it instead), but it was still very daring of Adrian to go for him. And I knew I was in good company when my old friend, Pete Postlethwaite, arrived to join me again. I have always been lucky as to the people I have worked with.

The first play Alan Rickman and I were in together was *Hamlet*, and we both had to double up. I played Marcellus and the Player Queen, and Alan played Laertes and the Player King. We had huge masks and wigs on and on one very memorable night, unfortunately with Alan Bates in the audience, Rickman's expansive arm gestures just caught me and knocked my wig and mask off. Rickman is a giggler like me and he certainly saw the funny side. He was chortling away behind his mask. Neither of us could carry on so we drew that scene to a close.

At first, I was really happy in Bristol because Lesley showed what a wonderful wife and mother she was by bringing Chloe, Mark and Sophie down and making a home for us in a small flat. It was pretty grotty, but she made it look as homely and comfortable as possible and I was simply delighted for us all to be together. The only problem was that the landlord did not allow children to live in his flats so, whenever he came round, Mark and Sophie used to take Chloe out and hide in the little back garden, trying to keep the baby quiet. We spent one wonderfully cramped Christmas there when her family and my mum all came down to stay. It was like a barrack room with camp beds lined up everywhere. We had hardly any money but we were very happy. I was playing Idle Jack in *Dick Whittington* at the time, and Alan Rickman was King Rat. I'm sure that is where he first got his ideas for the Sheriff of Nottingham in *Robin Hood*. But the family moved back to London where our home was and I was in digs down there when tragedy struck.

Chloe was very strong when she was born and she was a wonderful baby, but her young life was tragically cut short by meningitis. When she died, it was the worst thing that had ever happened to me. Losing my dad had been dreadful, but at least he had had a life. Chloe had had just 16 months. Lesley and I were both devastated. She was such a lovely, bouncy little girl. She looked like me — chubby, but she was gorgeous with it.

It was my opening night in a play called *Small Change* by Peter Gill. Lesley always came down for my opening nights, but she had never left Chloe overnight before. Her mother and aunt came down to look after Chloe while Lesley made the trip down to Bristol. Chloe had a cold and, of course, people now know that that can be an early symptom of meningitis. But nobody had told us then.

The first night went very well and the following morning I had just gone out to get the papers to see what the reviews were like. We were pleased because they were very good. Suddenly, the phone rang. Somehow, a sort of sixth sense told me that this phonecall meant that something was wrong. It was our landlady, Mrs Deeson, who called us down. She was in a terrible state. She said simply, 'The theatre has just rung up and said one of your daughters has died.' The horrible thing was that we had two daughters and we didn't know which one it was.

Tragically, it turned out that Chloe's cold symptoms had became worse after we had left and my mother-in-law called the doctor in the middle of the night. A locum came out and said it was not serious. But she got worse so mother-in-law and auntie took her to St Thomas's Hospital at 8.00 am and her little heart stopped on the way there. At the hospital they managed to get her heart going again, but she died soon afterwards. Chloe was my first child and it was the most terrible experience of my life. I was destroyed. I felt like giving up the profession, I felt like giving everything up and Lesley was in a terrible state, absolutely dreadful. We went to see Chloe before she was cremated. We walked into the chapel of rest and poor Lesley completely broke down and went screaming into the street.

My brother Terry came racing over to be with us and then he went and told my mother. She was devastated. Chloe was her first grandchild and she was absolutely shattered. Lesley's parents were with us and it was a horrible time for us all. It goes against all logic, your child dying; you just automatically assume that you are not going to outlive your children. Lesley's mum and dad and my mum were all a great help to us then. We tried to comfort each other and get through it as best we could. She would have been 21 on 4 November 1997. We have got a recording of her on tape, and the sight of this little girl just starting to walk always reduces me to tears whenever I see it.

It was dreadful for Lesley's mum when Chloe died. She and the aunt had been left in charge and she must have felt dreadful. But she did everything she could. She called the doctor and then rushed Chloe to the hospital first thing the next morning. Lesley's mum was absolutely distraught at the experience and very kind afterwards.

We were so broke at the time that my father-in-law actually paid for the funeral. We were absolutely skint. He is really a very kind man and I remember asking him for help. I suddenly had to make all these awful decisions myself, and I was asked if Chloe was to be cremated or buried. Lesley was so devastated she couldn't even speak about it. But she wanted a lock of Chloe's hair and I didn't know if that was possible or not. I suddenly felt very alone. My dad was dead and I realised I had no one to turn to. I remember going into our back room at our maisonette and asking my father-in-law what to do. I just needed an older person to advise me. He was so upset he just turned round with tears in his eyes and said, 'I'm so sorry, Kevin. I don't know. I can't help you.' He had never had to deal with a death like this. I suddenly realised I was alone in this and I had to make the decisions. To this day, I wonder if I made the right decision to have Chloe cremated and her ashes scattered with my father's at Markeaton in Derby. We talked about it afterwards, and Lesley was still not sure if she would rather have had Chloe buried so there would be a grave to visit. But there was just

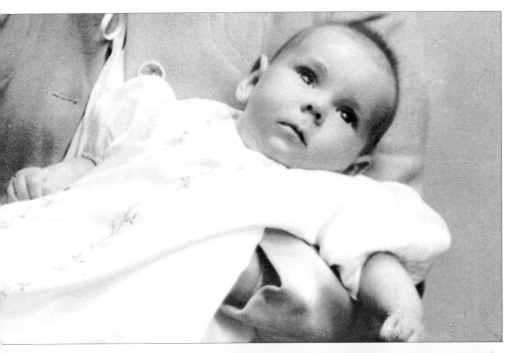

Top: What an angelic little chap! I was just three months old at the time.

Bottom: My dad was second from the right on the middle row, a proud member of the Derby Borough Police Force in 1950.

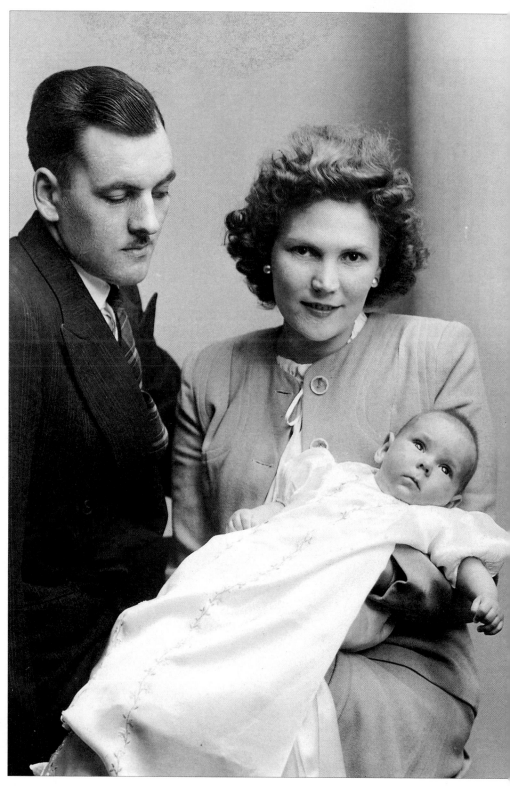

Above: In my mother's arms with my father looking on.

Opposite: Happy birthday to me. I loved cakes and even aged five I was on the way to getting fatter.

On holiday in Great Yarmouth, where we often stayed with my mum's relations. We're on my Uncle Ernie's boat.

Top: I tried to build my sand castles even with my wretched callipers on. We had the caravan right on the edge of the beach at Yarmouth. I used to shuffle down to the sea on my bottom. I was eight then. That's my mum and my brother Terry helping.

Bottom: A complete recovery. In my last year at primary school I was sportsman of the year and goalkeeper for the football team. I'm in the back row, third from the right.

I used to spend hours in front of the mirror trying to get my Cliff Richard quiff just perfect. The front tooth was kicked out in a football match.

op: With mum and dad on the Isle of Wight.

ottom: With Terry and mum and dad at Yarmouth.

Above: What a pair of legs! An open air performance of *Dick Turpin* at East 15 Acting School.

Opposite: A bit of a rogue... As Sam Gregory in *Dick Turpin*.

My first publicity photo taken just before I worked at the Royal Shakespeare Company for a season. Whatever happened to those cheekbones?

ritannia Hospital was a wonderful experience. Being frightening can be fun.

Top: As Don Watkins in *Coronation Street* in one of many scenes with Johnny Briggs as Mike Baldwin.

Bottom: Britannia Hospital, and that's a young and unknown Robbie Coltrane as the agitator on my left.

bove: So that's *What The Butler Saw*! Royal Court Theatre, London, 1975.

ottom: No trace of Tosh there – looking smooth as Les in *The Sea Anchor,* Liverpool
veryman Theatre, 1974.

What The Butler Saw! at the Whitehall Theatre.

ove: What a motley crew! As Grumio in *The Taming of the Shrew*, Liverpool Everyman
eatre, 1974. That's Matthew Kelly in the chef's hat.

tom: I met Kevin Kennedy on *Ducking Out*, and we went into *Coronation Street* together.

At the height of fashion! Tom in *The Pig and The Junkle*, Liverpool Everyman Theatre, 1975.

nobody to help me. I did get a lock of her hair and it is very moving because, as the years go by, the hair changes colour so you can see how her hair would have altered over the years.

I felt deeply sorry for my father-in-law over that period. It made me suddenly grow up and realise that, when it comes down to it, you are ultimately on your own in this world.

The actress June Brown — or Brownie as I always call her — better known to millions as Dot Cotton from *EastEnders*, became a dear and very important friend to me at that time. We had already palled up as we were sharing the same digs, and I would often perch on her bed and share a drink and talk long into the night. I'd get some whisky and she would be smoking her 900th cigarette of the day and we would just talk about life. She is a wonderful lady. The strange coincidence was that she had lost a child, also called Chloe, years before. She had already told me that a few days before my Chloe died. She was there to share my grief and there is a bond between us that lasts to this day.

Before that, Mark and Sophie had called me Uncle Kev. And for no apparent reason, after Chloe's death they started to call me 'Daddy'. We hadn't said anything to either of them about it. When they heard us crying they were so sweet; they came in and said to us, 'Don't cry Mummy and Daddy, Chloe's gone to God, she's very happy now.' That was the kids' innocence, which made us cry all the more.

In a way, I believe that is really why we ended up with so many kids because although we both knew perfectly well that you can never replace a child, Chloe's brothers and sisters are the nearest things to her. Even Elly now talks about her little sister Chloe who has gone away.

Most of my memories of the children growing up are so happy. I always used to play Santa Claus at the kids' primary school in London. All the kids would come up and I'd say, 'Well, little boy, what do you want for Christmas from Santa Claus?' One bright lad replied, 'A toy engine, Mr Lloyd.' I said, 'I'm not Mr Lloyd, I'm Father Christmas.' 'No you're not,' he said, 'you're Mark and Sophie's dad.' So much for my acting ability, I thought.

James came along some time afterwards. It seemed ages. People said that when you've lost a child, you have plenty of time to have more, but it doesn't seem like that and every month passed so slowly. We were both desperately keen to have more children. It seemed like an eternity, but, in fact, he was on his way a few months later.

I was at James's birth which was the most nerve-racking of all of them because we were so worried after Chloe's death. We had tried desperately to have another baby but, until you do, it's extra difficult somehow. You're still grieving for the child you've lost as well as trying to have another baby. We tried very hard and it seemed to be a very long and painful period for us, but it was actually only three months. I know it takes some people years of agony, but I can only say that three months seemed more like three years to me. I was so happy when I found out that Lesley was pregnant again and so was she. The two months we missed out had us in an awful turmoil.

James was the most worrying birth because we were so terrified that something would go wrong. Lesley went to one of her antenatal clinics and she happened to mention that she had had an X-ray on her teeth for some dental work. A stupid doctor there told her that if he had known that, he would have advised a termination! To be told that after you have just lost a child is very shocking. Lesley and I were in a terrible state. We asked our doctor, of course, and she said, 'Oh, don't be so silly, that's ridiculous.'

Lesley was about two weeks overdue with James and she had to be induced. It was just the most wonderful feeling because it was a blessing that we had a boy. He was very precious to us, just like they all are, but because of Chloe we had that extra worry about him. We used to wake up regularly in the middle of the night and go to check that he was still breathing. He was the most difficult of the lot because he had three months of colic, which was not diagnosed. He never stopped crying and he was extremely active. It seemed as though we never slept for the first three months.

Then, very soon after she had James, Lesley became pregnant with Pops, James was 18 on 27 May 1997, and Pops is 17 on 18 October. Hers was the funniest birth. Again, Lesley was induced. I was at St Thomas's all day waiting for her to come. I had been there for about six or seven hours and there was no sign of Poppy's arrival. They gave Lesley an epidural and told me, 'Go and have something to eat, Mr Lloyd, because she will be another four or five hours before she gives birth.' So I reluctantly went off in search of food.

As it was a Sunday, the hospital canteen was shut, so I walked across Westminster Bridge to a café. That became a sort of good luck thing with all my babies; I had a cup of tea and a sausage sandwich each time. But this time I was away for just 20 minutes. I know that because I was concerned about not being too long so I timed it. When I left the delivery room, it was packed with doctors and nurses and Lesley was lying there in some discomfort. When I came back 20 minutes later, they told me to wait in the waiting room but I just couldn't. I went into Lesley's room just to see for myself that everything was all right, but it was completely empty of people, apart from Lesley lying there on her own.

She looked totally washed out. She looked at me and said, 'I've had it... I've had it.' There was a little room next door where they bath the babies so I went in there to investigate. I was met with a large midwife who had a little baby in her hands, a little black baby. I was so choked with emotion that I blurted out, 'Is that mine?' She said, 'Now don't be so stupid, Mr Lloyd, yours is over there.'

I was so anxious that I wouldn't have been in the least surprised if they'd told me my baby was black. It was only much later that I thought to ask if we'd had a boy or a girl. We had to decide what to call her and it became a choice between India and Poppy. The *Daily Mail* came to take a photograph of Lesley and Poppy because Poppy was born on 18 October, Lesley was born on 18 October and her dad was born on 18 October. A remarkable hat-trick of family birthdays.

The reporter suggested that we give her a name there and then, and she suggested India. But Poppy was being looked after by a lovely Indian nurse so we didn't think it would really be suitable. So we decided on Poppy. It was quite appropriate really, because she came into this world in seven minutes, so she literally popped out.

There was about the same period of time before Henry was born on 5 July 1982. I had to help at the birth because there was a strike on. Again, it was a Sunday. Henry is the joker of the family. I'm the one in the entertainment business but he is much more naturally funny than I could ever be, so if anybody is going to take after me, it's likely to be him. It was probably my assistance at the birth which has made him so daft — I must have bumped his head on the way out. There were no doctors around so the midwife became the doctor and I became the midwife. If I was ever going to faint then that would have been the time, but it all went well.

We then had a bit of a child-free gap. We hadn't planned for any more, but we got a wonderful surprise when, seven years later, Edward appeared. He was born in Derby City Hospital. We were both delighted, and there wasn't even an initial bit of concern. Lesley just woke up one morning and wondered when her period should have started and, as I was better at dates than her, it suddenly clicked that it was a week late. I was delighted that Edward was born at the same hospital as me, the City Hospital in Derby.

Edward took ages to be born. Lesley went in initially with labour pains one evening when she thought things were happening, but Edward wouldn't budge. We were told to walk round the hospital to encourage him out. We walked for hours and in the end I had to sit down. I was absolutely knackered. Lesley was still going strong but I had to have a rest. Finally, we had to go home and he appeared about two days later. I was shattered.

I was in the West End at the time doing a play with Nicholas Lyndhurst called *The Foreigner* at the Albery Theatre, but I wasn't going to miss the birth so my understudy went on. Nicholas is a nice bloke and a very talented actor. I can't say I am surprised that he has gone on to such enormous comedy success. He always took it far more seriously than I did. He's not a gregarious bloke, not someone you can sit and chat with easily, but he is brilliant at being funny. You can't make him laugh, though, when he's working. I have a habit of trying to corpse people every now and then just to make life interesting, but I always failed with Nick. He was always much too controlled, too much of a consummate professional.

Tom Watt took over when he moved on and while he wasn't quite as good in the part, he never stopped laughing. He was a terrible giggler. Tom is a big Arsenal fan, so one night I set a special trap for him. That day in the paper there had been a story about my team, Derby, hoping to sign a player called Perry Groves from Arsenal. I was playing Tom's character's French friend in this strange play. Tom was already finding it difficult to keep a straight face even before then. Early on, we had to get a map out and I had to point to a place with a Russian-sounding name. That night, to keep Tom on his toes, I switched it to PerryGroveski. Naturally this meant nothing at all to the audience, but Tom exploded with laughter. We had 30 minutes to get through with just the two of us on stage, and every time I spoke to him he burst out laughing. I think it was pretty baffling for the audience.

The theatre always seemed to bring out the mischievous side of me but there were people who behaved far worse. One of my most bizarre memories is of appearing for director Mick Okrent in *Ducking Out*, Mike Stott's version of Edwardo de Philippo's original. Warren Mitchell was the star. Leslie Sands was also in it and Diane Bull played the daughter in this odd farce about a Catholic family. She was married to a butcher played by Phillip McGough and I was the lover, a bloke called Vincent. Kevin Kennedy was also there playing the son, but the reason it is etched on my brain is the performance given by Alan Devlin, an award-winning

Irish actor with a peculiar talent for surprising people —
especially his fellow actors. Early on, Kevin Kennedy
and I were going for a drink after rehearsals and we
asked Alan to join us. 'Oh no,' he said firmly. 'I don't
drink at all.'

We took him at his word, which turned out to be the
exact opposite of the truth. Then Devlin started having a
fling with one of the company, so he began getting all
emotional, although we did not know this was the
reason at the time. There were three acts, and Devlin
didn't come on until the last act, which was then just
about him on his own until the end. Warren Mitchell's
character had had a stroke by then and was left lying in
bed unable to speak coherently. But it was all Devlin's
act as he burst in as leader of this eccentric Irish family
from downstairs. One night, before the show, he came in
and seemed to be talking rather strangely. He wasn't
obviously drunk, it was just that his voice showed some
signs of bottle fatigue. He was full of the news that he
had just been offered a part in a film with Jack
Nicholson, which impressed the rest of us. Kevin and I
were upstairs talking in my dressing-room as the third
act opened.

Devlin walked on stage at The Duke of York Theatre
in front of just over 1,000 people. He said his first line
which was the abrupt question, 'What?' Then he walked
to the front of the stage and launched into a foul-
mouthed tirade about how there was no point in putting
on this stupid play. He said to the audience, 'I'm bored,
I'm f******* off to the pub for a drink. I should do the
same if I were you.' He was as good as his word, as he
turned on his heel and walked straight off the stage, out
of the theatre and into the pub. The first thing we heard
about the event were frantic messages for us to come to

the stage half-an-hour early to try to cobble together an ending out of the huge hole Devlin had left in the play. Leslie Sands was a real old pro and he held it together brilliantly and saved the day. Warren couldn't speak because his character had had a stroke. Leslie said, 'Ah, I think I can hear the doctor.' Renu Setna was playing the doctor and he wasn't due on for about another 20 minutes, but Leslie marched into the wings and grabbed him, saying, 'You're on,' and dragged him into the scene. Renu was supposed to examine Warren but he hadn't brought his stethoscope, so he sort of mimed the actions. I have never seen such frightened expressions as the ones on the faces of Diane Bull and Kevin Kennedy. We just didn't know what on earth was going on. Mind you, I had friends in that night and I am not at all sure that they really noticed that anything had gone wrong. They just thought it was rather a strange ending.

Later that night, we went over to the pub and found Devlin firmly installed at the bar, still in his full costume. We went up to him and he looked at us and said, 'I suppose you don't like me now.' We were just amazed and Kevin Kennedy and I took our drinks to the furthest end of the bar. Later, the management made an announcement. They were terribly sorry for what happened: 'Mr Devlin is obviously ill. We propose to send him home to Dublin for three weeks to get over it. His understudy will take over for that time.' Dublin of all places. What a city to send someone to, to forget about the drink! We were asked if we agreed to this course of action, and we did, even though Leslie Sands was not too keen. Devlin's understudy was dreadful and the play suffered because Devlin had been very good in the part. When he came back, it was grovelling and profuse apologies all round. 'It will never, ever happen again,' he told us all.

Then after 10 days, he went one better — he was so out of it he didn't even reach the stage. He arrived and demanded to see the company manager. The manager was terrified of Devlin.

'Yes, Mr Devlin?' he said nervously.

'You know this f****** play I'm supposed to be doing tonight?'

'Yes, Mr Devlin.'

'Well, I'm not,' Devlin said and just stormed off into the night. And it didn't even finish there. Two weeks later, the show went up late because there was an intruder who had broken into the theatre wearing a huge duck mask with a long beak. It was Devlin. He went up to the highest balcony and prepared to barrack us before he was escorted out by the police. Alan Devlin was certainly quite a character. And after all that, he still rang me up and asked me to his 40th birthday party. He was a lovely bloke with a bit of a wild streak to him.

CHAPTER SIX

HAPPY FAMILIES AND HARD WORK

My happiest memories are all from those days when the children were younger. We were often very hard up but we always made sure we had family holidays. In the beginning, we didn't have any money at all and the first holidays we went on were to St Ives in Cornwall. We used to rent a caravan and have the most marvellous times together. We were always poor because I was still in rep. I would just struggle to save up maybe £200 and we'd rent a caravan for a week or two and get away from it all. But we had wonderful times. I know I'm not exactly the first person to say this, but money definitely doesn't bring happiness. We just had great times.

The first place we moved to in late 1976 was a

maisonette. Lesley was brilliant at that because I had become a roving actor, a sort of vagabond with no great inclination to settle down in one place and be sensible. So, largely through Lesley's determination, we bought our little house for £11,000. We put £1,100 down and we had our first home. It was terrific, 21B Rosenau Road, just by Battersea Park, which for years I would use to run round to keep fit with actor friends of mine like Brian Glover and Alun Armstrong. We all spent a lot of time in the park because we had no garden for the kids to play in but I have only happy memories of the place. We had lovely times in the park.

St Ives had always been our holiday destination in the early years, but then we progressed and went to Salcombe and liked it very much. I bought a static caravan there and we enjoyed some tremendous holidays in it. In the evenings, we used to go down to the quay and have fish and chips, and just look at the boats. I remember one night a great big gull came down and pinched James's fish and flew away. There were tears from James and I had to go and buy him another one. Those were just lovely times; we were a close family who really enjoyed each other's company.

We also ventured to France a couple of times. That was a real adventure, loading up the car and driving through France with everyone boiling hot in the van. We had a Volvo Estate and there were always loud and lengthy arguments about who would sit in the back. Then, later, we had a van. We could never really have a normal family car, we just needed more space than a normal family. Sometimes it felt as though we were filming a new version of Cliff Richard's *Summer Holiday*. We loved it.

After the maisonette, we bought a house; 8 Atherton

Street, Battersea. We got it at an auction when it was a complete wreck and we paid £27,000. We sold the maisonette for £33,000 and moved to have more room. It was a big, happy house and I spent about another £25,000 having it done up by builders I knew. That was murder. I spent most of my time turfing the builders out of the pub. It was unbelievable. They used to arrive in the morning still shaking from the night before, hardly able even to drink a cup of tea at 10.00 am. And as soon as the boozers opened, they said they'd have to go and have a livener and that lasted until about 3.00 pm. They would then come back too drunk to do anything. When we first moved in, the cowboy builders hadn't finished anything properly so we were living in a quarter of the house.

It was terraced and needed complete refurbishment. We had four bedrooms, and to help pay the bills we had a lodger all the time we were there. We eventually sold it for £88,000 when we moved up to Derbyshire.

I do my acting by instinct. I love Shakespeare, and other playwrights like Chekhov and Ibsen, and sometimes I can have fascinating conversations long into the evening about the intricacies of a particular part, but generally it is not something that obsesses me. I am not precious about acting and I'd prefer to talk about football any day. People expect me to be this Kevin Lloyd, the actor chap, and I do not know who he is supposed to be — I'm just me.

Lesley and the family were always much, much more important to me than my career. Whenever people were becoming precious in the theatre or things became heated in a studio, I only had to think of Lesley and the children for all work problems to pale into insignificance. Acting has always been a great way to make a living but it has never been my life. My wife and family are my life. I was very, very lucky like that. Lots of people I have worked with do not have that background, and I saw that career set-backs would hit them that much harder. I am fortunate enough never to have had that many bad reviews, but when I have been knocked it never mattered that much. Without the wonderful love and support of Lesley and the kids, I would never have got where I am today. They were the rock that I relied on.

The very first telly I did was a children's thing called *Words and Pictures*. Bob Hoskins started off in it as well. It wasn't going to change the world, you understand, but it got me going in television. Unfortunately, it ended up with me getting glass in my eye and ending up in St Thomas's Hospital. There was a scene where I was one of two useless removal men, Bob and Ben the Removal Men, who had to wreck a house because of their incompetence. It involved smashing a ladder through a window, which is when some of the glass got into my eye. It was agony for a time but it was eventually removed at St Thomas's. That hospital has played a big part in my life.

I was in the very last episode of *Z-Cars*. I played a young killer who stabbed Tony Haygarth to death in the toilets. It was the start of a strange relationship between Tony and me. I have subsequently killed him three times in different roles. We always joke about it whenever we are cast together because I keep killing him and he keeps coming back for more. It's become a joke between us. Every time I meet him he says, 'How are you going to kill me this time?'

I killed him most memorably in *The Borgias* — mind you, I killed about eight people in six episodes and then they beheaded me on Christmas Day. I was Ramiro de Lorca, the paid assassin of Cesare Borgia, and I had the biggest wig, and the biggest codpiece in the whole production. I was very proud. It was a bit hard being topped on Christmas Day, but at least I was able to watch from a safe distance as, fortunately, they used a dummy for that scene. Nick le Prevost and I watched my grisly end while drinking brandy in a beautiful Italian village square. Sadly, the series was a flop for the BBC, but filming in Italy was wonderful — except when I went shopping, because with my long wig, which was too elaborate to take off, I was treated like a smelly hippie.

I enjoy all the soaps up to a point, but *Coronation Street* has always been my favourite. Back in 1978, I almost landed a part that would have changed my life. It was between me and a young actor called Chris Quinten to play a biker called Brian Tilsley. Many years later, I told Helen Worth, who plays Brian's long-suffering wife Gail so brilliantly, that I could have been her husband and she laughed and said jokingly, 'I wish you had been.'

But that was how I first came to the *Street*'s attention, and they kept me in mind. When they saw a part that was suitable they got in touch and offered me the role of Don Watkins in 1983. Don was Manager of the Graffiti Club and he was a real spiv, a great guy who was always ducking and diving and going for the main chance.

It was a new experience for me and I loved the cheerful camaraderie of a regular serial. It was strange in another way as well because, although I'm just 5ft 8in tall, I found myself towering over the guy I had a lot of my scenes with — Mike Baldwin. It was a new experience for me looking down on anyone. I was quite a lot taller than Johnny Briggs in spite of his Cuban heels. We used to do scenes in the bar and he'd be standing on his tiptoes. But he could laugh about it and we got on very well.

It was a very successful part and they asked me to stay on, but I was offered a film with Terence Stamp and at that time I opted for that classic actor's attitude of 'Oh no, I don't want to get type-cast in a soap', even if it was and still is an amazingly successful show.

Kevin Kennedy, who plays Curly Watts, and I are old friends. We joined *Coronation Street* at exactly the same time. We had just worked together in the West End in *Ducking Out*. It was around the time of the big exit of Len Fairclough and the *Sun* came up with a big feature on 'Who is gonna save Coronation Street?' and there was a line-up of around 10 or 15 new characters. They gave them all *Sun* ratings, a star ability, and I was delighted when I came second with eight out of ten. Tracie Bennett just beat me with nine. Curly only got four, although he's still there and doing very well.

Don Watkins was a smashing character. In fact, when he disappeared with £5,000 of Mike Baldwin's money, Terry Wogan had his 'Spot the Don Watkins' campaign and a load of people rang in saying they'd seen me. It went on for weeks. People used to come up to me in the street and say, 'We've spotted you,' and then ring up Wogan. I was asked to go back, but I thought the film would be the start of bigger things, and I also had the actor's worry that stopped me wanting to be there for life.

Leaving was a difficult decision to make, but I thought that the film with Terence Stamp might be really big. I was frightened of being type-cast in a soap. I know I've gone on to become a regular in *The Bill*, but that's not a soap, and I'm also quite a bit older now and maybe a little more realistic.

Every year, Kevin tells me he is going to leave, but then a letter comes and he's got another reason to stay. It's human nature and I don't blame him at all, but every year he tells me he's leaving. I admire people like Sarah Lancashire who go on to other things.

I got on very well with Liz Dawn, and got to know her family as well. I can remember one day waiting at the Rovers bar to do a scene after lunch with Barbara Knox who plays Rita. Liz wasn't there and all of a sudden the door crashed open and Liz burst in absolutely roaring with laughter. Barbara said, 'Here we go again,' and everyone laughed. I was still a young lad then and very impressionable. I loved scenes with Barbara because she was very good and very professional.

After the *Street*, I became very friendly with Pat Phoenix, who played Elsie Tanner for years. We did a comedy series together called *Constant Hot Water*. She was very much larger-than-life — a real star, not a fake. She understood her audience intimately and she was also a very kind lady. At that time, there was a sort of war of the queens, because Barbara Knox was vying with Pat in the heyday of Elsie Tanner. There was a great deal of competition between Barbara and Pat. But they were both consummate actresses. They both had very strong parts which they played very well and the competition worked well for the series.

I remember Bill Roache was very generous in his praise of my work and he begged me to stay on. He was generous enough to say that they were desperately short of good, strong male characters, which I think is still the case today. He even went to the producers and asked them if I could be asked to stay. He was right when he pointed out that there were plenty of strong women but not many strong men. The show is based on strong women, and always has been.

They were very happy days. The first day of work on *Coronation Street* was quite daunting. I remember it being a Sunday, and I was directed to the rehearsal room. Even if you've done loads of work before, it's frightening. You go up the stairs and open the door and you're confronted by all these famous faces of people you feel you really know, who have been regularly in your living-room for 30 years. And suddenly you're in the middle of them.

I can remember the producer's run being one of the most nerve-racking things to go through. As a newcomer, I was scared to death of making a mess of it. They were all extremely kind and made me feel at home. I have worked on some series where people didn't even bother to say 'hello'. That's why I always make a point of introducing myself to the guest actors in *The Bill*.

After the first episode of the *Street* had gone out, all of a sudden I was public property. We were on holiday in St Ives and I would be stopped all the way up and down the street by people who had seen Don Watkins arrive the night before.

I based Don on a flash guy I knew from Derby, who was a bouncer at one of the night clubs. I had a lot of scenes with Hilda Ogden and was amazed, like everyone else who met her, at how different the kind, soft-spoken Jean Alexander was from her interfering character. You wouldn't recognise her in a million years and she wouldn't thank you to either.

Johnny Briggs took me under his wing and often invited me back to his flat for meals. Johnny was very aware of the dangers of taller actors dwarfing him. He's been right up on tiptoes for some scenes, but he's still so small he can't look many people in the eye. But he's a good bloke, Johnny. Big in more important ways, like his personality.

Most people on *Coronation Street* were very generous — apart from Fred Feast, who played barman Fred Gee, that is. On one of my first days at Granada, Johnny Briggs took me for a drink after work and we went into the bar just behind Fred. He ordered five pints and I thought, 'That's nice of him, he's getting the drinks in.' But he went on to ferry all five pints over to a table in the corner and sat down on his own. I was puzzled, but Johnny explained: 'You weren't hoping to get a drink out of Fred, were you? They're all for him. He doesn't believe in buying drinks for anyone else.'

One of my favourite showbusiness friends is Victoria Wood, and I was so pleased to get a part in the play *Talent*, that really seemed to launch her as a performer as well as a writer. In the television adaptation I played the flash compère of the grotty talent competition. It was a part played on stage by a chap called Eric Richard, whom I have since got to know pretty well as Sergeant Bob Cryer in *The Bill*. *Talent* was a beautifully written piece of work and I enjoyed every minute of working with Victoria. She did give me a surprise early on, though, when she invited me out to dinner to meet her husband and he turned out to be none other than my old friend Geoff Durham. I really must try to read the papers more.

In those days, I was very wary about becoming type-cast, so after a very successful year I decided it was time to move on. Just as I was leaving the Street, I got the offer of a part that simply made my head spin with delight. The phone rang one night at home. Lesley answered it and shouted, 'It's Lindsay Anderson for you.' He started full of small-talk and then asked casually, 'What are you up to at the moment, old chap?' I explained that I was just finishing in the *Street*. He said, 'What are you doing from January onwards?' He had previously tried to get me to play a marvellous role, that of Yasha in Chekhov's *The Cherry Orchard*, but I had been unavailable. He reminded me of this and said 'We're doing it again. We're taking it to LA and this time I'd like you to come with us and play Yasha.' I had my hand over the phone in an instant and I was yelling with glee to Lesley, 'I'm going to America. I'm going to America.' Lindsay went on to say that he had had to re-cast quite a few parts and he said, 'I've got to rehearse the old boy in it, because he has taken over from Bernard Miles, playing the part of Firs, the old retainer.'

I listened intently, wondering who on earth 'the old boy' was, but not wishing to give away my lack of knowledge. Lindsay went on and said, 'The old boy wonders if you would spend a couple of weeks at his house before rehearsals begin, going over all the scenes you have together. It would help him greatly.'

'Of course,' I said,

'You live in Battersea, don't you?' Lindsay asked. 'Well, the old boy lives in Chelsea, so it's not very far away, is it? You would be prepared to travel wouldn't you?'

'Yes,' I said, a bit bemused.

'Oh, Larry will be pleased.' He just dropped it in like that. He knew very well that Olivier was my hero. All of a sudden, the penny dropped. I said, 'Lindsay, who exactly is the old boy?'

'Oh, Larry Olivier, Kevin. Is that all right with you?'

I was walking on cloud nine. In the next few weeks, I

got my permission from American Equity through, as well as the money and all the details of the hotels and rehearsals. Lesley was already choosing what she was going to wear. The show was going to LA for three months and then it was going to Broadway. I could hardly wait. We were about three weeks away from starting when I was at the headquarters of Central TV, tying up the details of a children's TV role which would fill the time before we started perfectly. Everything in my life was going well. Too well. I came out thinking 'Life is sweet'. As I walked out, I heard an *Evening Standard* vendor shout, 'Read all about it. Lord Olivier seriously ill in hospital.' I just wandered along in a dream and bought the paper. All the awful details were there; he had been rushed in. The following day I received the phone call from the production office. Without Lord Olivier there was no production. What a miss. I had been given a chance to work with my God, something beyond my wildest dreams. I'd have given anything for that and then to have it snatched away at the last minute was almost too hard to bear. It was the major miss of my life.

Soon afterwards, Lindsay was in touch again, trying to team up Brian Glover and me again, this time as two window cleaners in his film *Britannia Hospital*. He loved to work with people from his personal stable and we all had very fond memories of *What the Butler Saw*. I was working at the Royal Shakespeare Company at the time doing *Love Girl and The Innocent* by Solzhenitsyn, which involved having my head shaved. But the dates clashed and I thought I had lost the chance to appear in the film until Lindsay called again. Tony Haygarth had dropped out and there was a wonderful part of an intimidating, shaven-headed brute called 'Scalp-Cut' up for grabs. On paper it wasn't that much, but he seemed to be in the action quite a bit. He was picketing the gates and frightening everyone to death and then, later on, raiding the hospital. It became a wonderful part. My threatening shaven head stuck out and I lead the whole revolt. Lindsay wrote me a brilliant letter afterwards saying what a fortunate twist of fate that I couldn't play the original role, leaving me free for this much more dominant part. Scalp-Cut worked really well.

My second-in-command was Robbie Coltrane, who was totally unknown then. I think I had about ten lines in the film and Robbie had about three. But he was smashing. And, somehow, I think I knew then that he was going places. He had such an amazing presence about him I thought he might do well, so it is no surprise to me that he became a huge star. He was wonderful at entertaining the troops, clowning and playing the piano while we were hanging round for all that time they seem to waste on film sets. We became good friends, Robbie and I. My third-in-command leading the mob was an actor called Robert Pugh. Coltrane was so taken with the group that he was going to write a comedy for the three of us.

There was one hilarious moment in the film when a tremendous older actor, Graham Crowdon, playing the boss of the hospital, had to drive through the pickets in a determined bid to get to work. He was supposed to stop when I ran in front of him. But Graham would admit himself that he is not a very good driver, and when it came to the take, in front of Friern Barnet Mental Hospital where we were filming, he did not stop. He went straight through me. Luckily I was very fit in those days, so when I realised what was happening, I rolled on to the bonnet and off the side and was able to carry on with the scene. My thigh was badly bruised but the scene looked very realistic and it was edited into the film. All Graham could say afterwards was, 'It's all right. I knew he would get out of the way somehow.'

Joining the RSC was always one of my main ambitions when I left drama school. I was later asked by Adrian Noble when he joined to stay for two seasons, but it would have been in Newcastle and Stratford-upon-Avon and I didn't want to uproot the children at that time so I sadly decided to turn them down. He offered me some wonderful parts. I was going to be in Kenneth Branagh's *Henry V* and Anthony Sher's *Richard III*, but I felt that the 15-month contract would have meant too much upheaval for the children and I didn't want to be away from them for that long.

I have almost always been lucky in the people I have worked with — not only actors but brilliant directors like Lindsay Anderson, Mike Okrent, Alan Dossor, Joan Littlewood and Stephen Frears. Stephen's a lovely bloke. He comes from Leicester, so we agreed we were fellow Midlanders when we worked together on a television play by Mike Stott called *The Last Company Car*. There was a part as a policeman, one which seems to have followed me throughout my career. I was offered the part very late, probably because someone had dropped out. I was playing opposite the wonderful Jim Broadbent. I was a Sergeant and grew my moustache for the first time and mutton chop sideburns as well. It ended with us being locked in an electric garage and Broadbent's character had a heart-attack. The rest of the company wanted to decide between us for the most over-the-top performance, because we were both verging on insanity. It was a wonderful time. But for that final scene, Stephen Frears went for that extra bit of realism and locked us in the garage for real, with him and a cameraman. He just said, 'Right. That's it. We're not leaving here until we get this right.' Some of us became very claustrophobic as the time ticked on.

Later, Jim and I did a pilot with Alfred Molina for a comedy series called *Oysters,* written by Stan Hey. He had written my part, Harry Blackburn, the country and western music fan, in *Auf Wiedersehen, Pet.*

Years after I had first met him on the film *Trial by Combat,* I found myself working with the great Sir John Mills again in an ATV series called *Young at Heart.* Sir John starred alongside Megs Jenkins who played his wife and I played his son, who sadly emigrated to Australia after a couple of episodes. But it was a privilege to work with one of our great theatrical knights and to be impressed again by his fitness and love of life which belied his years. He was a real gent and I'll never forget the time at a big reception after filming when he was being ushered hither and thither to meet dignitaries. He put his foot down and made a point of coming over to meet Lesley. It was wonderful of him because he came over and said, 'I've worked with your husband now for weeks and he is a marvellous actor.' He was a very kind man to work with.

My most recent appearance with that fine actress Gwen Taylor was at Pride Park, the new home of my beloved Derby County, when we were both guests at the official opening by HM The Queen in July 1997. We both have Derby in common, and she also comes from Alvaston. I followed her to the amateur dramatic group Derby Theatre in the Round, and then to the East 15 acting school some years later. Gwen is a real pal and we worked together in a series about a Derbyshire brass band called *Sounding Brass,* written by the Derbyshire playwright Don Shaw. Brian Glover also starred in it, and although it was a great show, it was unfortunately a victim of the ITV strike. It was wonderful to see Gwen again. Let's hope our football team soon give us something to celebrate.

The third production I worked on with Lindsay Anderson was *The Playboy of the Western World* for Albert Finney's company, United British Artists. We started off at the Oxford Playhouse and then went up to the Edinburgh Festival, and then transferred to the Riverside. Lindsay made me play a wheedling Irish nephew, a part totally alien to me. The accent was very difficult for me and I told Lindsay of my problems. He just said, 'It will be very good for you to do, Kevin. I'm sure you'll be brilliant.' I just didn't like the character at all but Lindsay coaxed a good performance out of me and I managed to get very good reviews. What was even more remarkable was when my mother came to see it with Lesley — she didn't recognise me. I had been on stage for about a quarter-of-an-hour when my mother asked Lesley when I was going to come on.

It was all down to Lindsay. He was a great director. He taught me how important it was to be truthful in your acting and I have always remembered that. Nothing else matters as much as that. And Lesley always helped me. She used to do the lines with me for all my parts, and I also enjoyed doing lines with the kids. Poppy was very good; she used to love doing the panto lines with me. Then when I had a song to do, the kids beat a retreat because I'm not the greatest singer in the world. I had to attempt the baddie's song from *The Lion King* for my role as the villain in *Jack and the Beanstalk* at the Birmingham Hippodrome. It took me ages to manage that song. I could never get it right so I used to sing it all over the house.

I loved doing *Auf Wiedersehen, Pet*. It was a marvellous series to work on. I became firm friends with Kevin Whately, Tim Healy, Timothy Spall and the amazingly unpredictable Jimmy Nail. I have never come across anyone quite like Jimmy Nail before or since. He is a class actor, but he can be a shade surprising to work with. We had a scene together that I will never, ever forget. It was all about country and western music because my character was Harry Blackburn, a music-mad plumber, specially written for me by Stan Hey, who first got Jimmy to sing on television. So I suppose you could say I've got a lot to answer for.

It was a long scene. We were sitting on a wall in a sort of typically extended lunch break. We both had to knock back the lager as we were talking and we did six or seven takes so we were both becoming fairly lubricated. Then Jimmy suddenly said, 'I'm going to eat this whole jar of pickled onions. No kidding.' I thought he was joking, so all the way through this scene he is eating pickled onions and my eyes were getting wider and wider all the time.

When we got to the end, we were supposed to go 'Cheers' to each other and take a drink from a can of beer. But not Jimmy. He goes 'Cheers' and swigs back the jar of vinegar that the pickled onions had been in. If you watch that episode you can see that the expression of shock on my face was absolutely real. I just couldn't believe he'd done it — he drank it all. For me, there has never been an entrance to television quite like Jimmy Nail's portrayal of Oz in *Auf Wiedersehen, Pet*.

He was just so real and it came over on screen. He would always be wandering around scratching his balls and he wasn't going to let a little thing like television cameras stop him doing that. I got on with him very well, and later, when he became famous and a programme-maker himself, he asked me to be in *Crocodile Shoes*, but I was locked into *The Bill* and I had to decline.

Jimmy hates producers with a passion, but he is very good to fellow actors with the one notable exception of Gary Holton, who played the cockney wide-boy in *Auf Wiedersehen, Pet*. The only time I ever saw Jimmy get wound up by another actor was when Gary was always, always late. We inevitably had to wait for him. I remember staying at the George Hotel in Nottingham for one stretch of filming, and in the morning we would all have had our breakfast and be waiting on the bus, but there would still be no Gary. We would sit there and wait for 15 minutes or half-an-hour. Jimmy would get really wound up by this and, all of a sudden, you'd see Gary Holton coming down the road with some bird on his arm. Then, when we arrived at the location we often found that Gary Holton couldn't say a word because he'd been up all night. Poor Gary tragically died during filming of the second series, which cast a sad shadow over a wonderful show.

CHAPTER SEVEN

COMING HOME

We wanted to move away from London when Mark and Sophie, our two older children, were about to go to secondary school. We didn't think the secondary schools in London were very good and private schools were really out of the question because we couldn't afford them. I had always insisted on coming back to London where we had lived for 15 years, but we moved because of the children. We ended up with Mark at the age of 11 travelling 12 miles a day to go to Holland Park Grammar school. For a young schoolboy that's not ideal. We also felt that we'd had enough of the city — Lesley fancied being surrounded by countryside, and so did I.

I come from Derby so I knew the area. We decided to

take the risk and we went straight to Duffield, specifically to be in the catchment area of Ecclesbourne School. As a schoolboy I used to play rugby for Bemrose and for the county, and although we were county champions, Ecclesbourne was the only school which really challenged us. I remembered what a good school it was and I had heard that it had kept up its standards. It is still a fine school and all our children have gone there. The younger ones started at the Church of England school which is just up the road.

Lesley and I had both had enough of London. We looked at Brighton first. I have always liked the place and there's a thriving actors' community there, but then we switched to Derby. My only fear about moving there was that it was too far away from London and I would be out on a limb, cut off from the profession up North. And I wasn't 100 per cent sure that that was what I wanted. But it felt as though it was the right time to move and the good rail line helped to convince us.

We came up one Saturday to look at houses in Duffield and, as soon as we walked into Stockbrook House, we loved it. As we were being shown around for the first time, the lady from the estate agent was just opening the back door to show us the back garden when Lesley turned to me and said, 'I love it.' And that was it. I felt just the same. We both knew it was the Lloyd family home, and that is why, when we broke up, I said to Lesley, 'Don't ever sell this house, the children love it,' and it has always had a wonderful family feeling.

Just like we fell in love with each other at first sight, we fell in love with the house instantly. They were asking £55,000 and I managed to negotiate it down to £52,000. And it was worth every penny. That was in 1985. We moved when I was working on the second series of *Auf Wiedersehen, Pet.*

When we got to Duffield we were both delighted. It made me wonder why I hadn't done it before. The kids were happier in the countryside, they had fresh air and more freedom, and we had a lovely house. Things were just right without the hustle and bustle of London. It had seemed that the teachers and parents had been obsessed with trying to stamp out bullying and cutting down on drugs, rather than the onset of 'O'-levels and 'A'-levels.

We always had big birthday parties, wore hats and blew out the candles. The house was never empty. Ben Roberts from *The Bill* came with his wife for one Christmas and he said he had never been in a house quite like it. He said, 'It's a real family house.' Kids and toys seemed to spill out all over the place. That is what I loved.

We always had just enough. We were never exactly hand-to-mouth but we never seemed to get ahead. The trouble, really, was that a lot of my work was in the theatre and the wages are so low for stage work that you virtually have to pay to do it, particularly if you're keeping a house on somewhere else; you need a private income.

Christmas was always a very special time. We used to have about 15 people for Christmas dinner, a complete houseful. I loved Christmas; it was a real family time. We often used to have lodgers from the Derby Playhouse staying with us, such as Simon Dutton who later married Lord Olivier's daughter, Tamsin. He always used to say that every time they opened a door, someone would appear. Lesley and I both loved a busy house. We both liked having plenty of guests, but Christmas was always special. There would be Lesley's family, my family, and plenty of friends. We would all have a lovely time in our wonderful, special house.

We didn't have a great deal of money for a long time. It was only when I landed the regular contract on *The Bill* that we started to find ourselves a bit better off. But we always enjoyed the simple things in life, like just being a family. We had rows like anyone else, but we had loads of happy times as well, basically because we were very close.

It was great. Lesley was totally supportive, and she didn't suffer from an inflated ego at all. I know if you're going out with an actor, any actor in a popular show, it must be irritating when people come up all the time and talk to them and ignore you. Just because they're on television. But Lesley always seemed to shrug that off. She recognised it as part of the job; she didn't mind. I know that causes a great deal of friction in a lot of actors' relationships. Being referred to as 'Kevin's wife' all the time can't have been easy but she never complained, she supported me and backed me all the way.

The most unhappy experience I've had in my professional career was a disastrous production of a play called *Balmoral* by Michael Frayn at The Bristol Old Vic. John McEnery was taken ill at the last minute and I was brought in to play the main part. We started off at Bristol, went to Cambridge and then transferred to the prestigious Singapore Arts Festival as Great Britain's entry.

I've never come across a cast like that, neither would I want to again. It just didn't gel, and the director, Leon Rubin, wasn't much help. Bristol Old Vic used to be one of the best and the happiest theatres outside London, but *Balmoral* was a nightmare for me from start to finish.

And I think it was only because I suffered the indignity of getting good reviews. The critics said it was the best comedy performance for months and my life was made hell from that moment on; some of the cast seemed to be so bitchy.

The cast included Bernard Lloyd, a man I have always regarded as a fine actor; Helen Ryan, who had won an award in the television series *Edward VII* playing Queen Anne; and the beautiful Lysette Anthony. I turned up for a read-through, and it was the first time I had seen the play. My part was as a strange Scottish gillie (a sort of valet) who doubles up as Sir Hugh Walpole. It was a comedy and that was how I played it. The first night was certainly a memorable experience. It was a bit unnerving and seemed to flash by. In fact, I looked a bit like Eric Morecambe in desperate search of Ernie Wise, although it seemed to go down well with the audience and I got loads of laughs. I'd been a bit nervous about arriving as a late substitute so I was relieved.

Then, as we were walking off the stage after the opening night towards our dressing-rooms, I encountered a somewhat suspicious Bernard Lloyd. He's an old Royal Shakespeare Company actor and is conscious of his status.

'What did you think Bernard?' I said. 'How do you think it went tonight?'

He looked at me as though I was something he had just stepped in, and said in his deep, Shakespearian voice, 'Well, boy, I don't know what you were playing at.'

'What do you mean?' I asked.

'You were playing to the gallery and I didn't like it at all.'

Then Helen Ryan hissed something rather unpleasant at me. I suddenly realised I was not their favourite person. Lesley was there and she heard all this, and as we got back into my dressing-room we looked at each other in real surprise. Slowly, their reactions registered and my anger grew. I said, 'Hang on a minute,' and I walked down to Helen Ryan's dressing-room and told her what I thought of her comments. I went on to Bernard Lloyd's dressing-room and gave him a mouthful. I was really livid.

When the reviews came out, I really was in trouble. I received rave notices, with one critic even commenting 'Kevin Lloyd is a comic genius'. The next day, I arrived back at the theatre to find the rest of the cast sitting around looking shell-shocked. I was still angry and stormed, 'Well, what do you expect? It is the main part.'

Soemone said imperiously to me, 'Bernard Lloyd is a man of enormous talent and experience. He is a man of 55 who has spent a lifetime perfecting his craft and he has only received one review.'

I couldn't resist it: 'Well, perhaps I was better than him,' I said cheekily, watching with delight as her face flushed with rage.

It was all very silly. There we were with a surprise success on our hands, and we were hardly speaking to each other. Bernard Lloyd did say it was, 'An incredibly popular, successful performance.'

At one point, I was so distraught I sat down in the Grand Hotel in Bristol and wrote a long letter to Lindsay Anderson. I was very down and I just sat there and let everything pour out on to the paper about how unhappy I was. He wrote me a long letter back. His basic response was: 'Take a deep breath and just accept it all as experience. Make the most of it and try to learn.'

Unfortunately, this all happened at the beginning of a run which was to take us to Cambridge and then

Singapore. The atmosphere was so bad that hardly anyone spoke to each other at all. The fact that Lesley came with me was the saving grace as far as I was concerned. I resigned three times during the run, but I was told that they couldn't let me go because the whole production was centred around me. The producers said they would sack the others if I would carry on, but I didn't want that on my conscience. I didn't want anybody to get sacked. I didn't want to carry on either, but Lesley talked me into sticking with it because if I hadn't, all I would have achieved would have been bad publicity for walking out of the play.

I was determined to pull out but Lesley was even more determined to see Singapore. We were out in the car one day arguing about what I should do, and we passed a phone box somewhere in the middle of the Derbyshire Moors. Lesley said, 'Stop the car. You're going to get out of this car now and you're going to ring the Bristol Old Vic and tell them that you are going to do that play in Singapore. Otherwise, I'm leaving you, honestly.'

'I'm not doing it,' I said, and we had a heavy discussion about the play.

'We can go to Singapore,' Lesley suggested, 'and we don't have to spend any time with them. We can be on our own but we're going, so get out of this car and ring them up now and tell them you're going.'

I did, and our trip to Singapore was confirmed.

Despite the director and constant disgruntlement from other members of the cast, we finally arrived in the Far East. One of the things that surprised me most was that I didn't think anyone would understand a word, but we went down a storm. The production was voted Best Play and I won an award for Best Actor. I was delighted. I just thought that I'd been vindicated.

Lesley and I used to go off on our own in Singapore, and spent most of our time just walking around. We went into the Raffles hotel to see where *Tenko* was filmed — it was Lesley's favourite television programme at the time. And we sampled several Singapore Slings. We were very happy. Back at the theatre, the atmosphere was becoming unbearable.

In spite of these setbacks, the production won the festival. We rang up Michael Fryan who was delighted and we came back smelling of roses. I've never been so happy as when we landed at Heathrow and were able to say goodbye to each other.

Back in England, I did two episodes of *Dear John*, the excellent Ralph Bates comedy written by the brilliant John Sullivan, the creator of such classics as *Only Fools and Horses* and *Citizen Smith*. I played the bizarre character Ricky Fortune, a rock singer who had split up from his wife, drank too much alcohol and took too much cocaine. It was a wonderful part and, in fact, the BBC did consider developing Ricky in his own series. While it was on television I was doing *Andy Capp* with James Bolam and it was a hugely enjoyable experience. He has got this reputation for being prickly, but that was the exact opposite of how I found him.

Whether he took to me because I was a young actor I don't know, but I just happened to say to him that my episodes of *Dear John* were on one night. Some time later, I got a message saying, 'James Bolam wants to see you in his caravan at one o'clock.' I wondered what I'd done, but when I turned up he said, 'I watched *Dear John*. You were brilliant. It was the best comedy I have seen on television for ages. What are you going to do with it? I'm going to ring John Howard Davies and get him to get you a comedy series.' The following day I got a message of congratulations from John Howard Davies, which was nice even if I didn't get the comedy series. I thought James Bolam had been really generous. Most actors wouldn't do that because they are so concerned about their own performances and their own futures.

The real stars are unique, like James Bolam, Jimmy Nail, Alan Bates or Albert Finney. They don't have to worry about anyone else. What James Bolam was doing was trying to set me up as a comedy actor who might have rivalled him in years to come, and that takes a big man to do it.

Alan Bates, along with Albert Finney, Laurence Olivier and Tom Courtney, is a great hero of mine. Lindsay Anderson introduced me to him when I was in the West End doing *What the Butler Saw*. Soon after, Alan Bates was doing *Otherwise Engaged* and I was walking through Soho when I saw him approaching. Because I'm a bit shy, I felt nervous about seeing my hero again and I walked over to the other side of the road. He then crossed the road to my side which surprised me. I just put my head down and looked away, attempting to walk past him. Then Alan Bates stopped me and said, 'You're Kevin Lloyd, aren't you?' It was like something out of a dream. My hero stopping me rather than the other way round. He said, 'I'm Alan Bates.'

Like a berk, I said, "Ooh, I know.'

'Well, we're both from Derbyshire, aren't we?' he said. He then invited me for coffee at the theatre where he was absolutely charming and we became friends. About 18 months later, he was in *The Seagull* at the Duke of York's Theatre and he invited me over again. I went with Lesley, who was heavily pregnant, into his dressing-room. Alan was changing his trousers behind a chair and looking quite embarrassed about it when he saw how pregnant Lesley was. He offered her the chair saying, 'We don't want you to have it here.'

There was a figure behind the door who suddenly stepped forward and dramatically offered Lesley a chair. 'Madame may sit down here. And Monsieur may sit down there.' Then Alan made the introductions and I realised that the guy asking us to sit was none other than Rudolph Nureyev. Alan said, 'Rudy–Kev, Kev–Rudy', just as though he was nobody. Alan is a lovely bloke with absolutely no selfishness about him. We meet in Ashbourne occasionally and I am always embarrassed because fans of *The Bill* recognise me and he, amazingly for one of our greatest actors, can proceed relatively unnoticed.

CHAPTER EIGHT

THE BILL

That great TV writer, Geoff McQueen, provided the name Tosh for me. I have never really known exactly where he got the name. I used to say to people that it comes from 'mackintosh', which the character nearly always wears, but I'm not sure of that. I think it's more likely that it's a cockney word for 'mate'. It certainly suits the character, though. Not many people know that his real name is, in fact, Alfred.

Geoff McQueen invented the whole series and Tosh was the last character he created. Any character after Tosh was dreamed up by script editors, producers or other writers, because Geoff sadly died soon afterwards. I had worked with Geoff on two Jim

Davison series, *Up the Elephant and Round the Castle* and
Home James. In *Home James* I was a copper and maybe it
was there Geoff McQueen saw some potential in me
joining the force for longer. I'd like to think so. In *Up
the Elephant* I was just a mate.

Jim Davison was great. He is genuinely, incredibly
funny. We have remained very close friends. Lesley
came to see a recording and her verdict was that he is
the funniest bloke you could ever wish to meet. I
remember in one scene that I had to burst into a
bedroom where he was in bed with a girl, and he had
been doing his own warm up which left the audience
laughing so much we couldn't do the scene.

He is very professional but he is also very generous.
He would suggest all sorts of alternatives, and hand
out priceless pieces of advice on timing. You always
got a bigger laugh if you did it his way. There are not a
lot of comics like that around.

But he also had a deeply upsetting habit of going
cross-eyed before a scene which would inevitably make
me laugh and get me into trouble with the director.

I have been involved with *The Bill* since 1988, a
quarter of my life. I wasn't in it right at the very start,
when it was just another crime series of hour-long
episodes. But when the producers decided to convert it
into a regular, half-hour series, they created a bigger
team to cope with the amazing workload.

I believe Geoff's description of the character he came
up with was based on me. He was late-30s, scruffy,
overweight, with a big family and couldn't pay the
mortgage. That was me to a tee.

I'm sure he wrote it specifically for me because after
one night's filming with Jim, Geoff said to me, 'I am
writing a police series and I'd like to write a part in it

for you.' I never thought anything else about it, and then Tosh came through the letterbox. As soon as I read it, I knew it was a part I simply had to play.

I grew my moustache for Tosh and it has become my trademark, but I don't think I would have it out of choice. I thought it would be a six-month thing, but now I've had the damn thing for nine years.

Tosh Lines has always been a tribute to my dad. When I put on the clothes, the crumpled mac and the shiny suit, I get an image of him in my mind. I start walking like him and even adopt some of his mannerisms.

I often get calls from his friends in the force who are now retired saying, 'You were just like your father last night on TV.' I have inherited some of his dark Celtic looks — and the same receding hair, I'm afraid. My dad's friends tell me that the character brings back a lot of fond memories for them and it does for me as well. He is still remembered at the Derbyshire Constabulary where he worked by young officers he trained, who are now often quite high-ranking. My dad was an excellent policeman and he was very well respected by his colleagues.

I base Tosh's caring nature and compassion on my dad. Tosh isn't the kind of copper who just wants to lock somebody up for the sake of it. Like my dad, he can be tough when it matters but he also cares about people, and I think that is a very important quality in a policeman. Tosh has also got a real policeman's instinct. He is the fellow the other officers go to when they are stumped by a problem. Dad had that gift of real insight, too.

The success of the show never fails to amaze me. Cop shows seem to come and go pretty regularly, but *The*

Bill is still around. We have won two major awards in the last few months and I enjoy it more than ever. I think it's now heading towards becoming the longest-running cop show ever. We have already achieved the most episodes, but the longest-running is the next landmark.

It is the natural successor to *Z Cars*. My old man thought *Z Cars* was the nearest thing you'd ever get to the real police force. I'm sure he would say the same about *The Bill*.

When I went up for the part in *The Bill*, there was another actor auditioning for it as well. I have always felt sorry for the guy who didn't get it because instant decisions and moments like that change your whole life. It was a bloke called Bill Moody who missed out and I've never seen him since. His name is lodged in my brain now.

It came down to the two of us for Tosh, and I thought, 'Poor sod, that could have been me.' But this time I was the lucky one. When they gave me the nod I rushed out to ring Lesley because it was something we both really wanted. We didn't know it would be as successful as it has become, but we knew it would be good regular money for a while and we certainly needed that at the time.

In a way, having a long contract and a regular working routine was like being back in the solicitors' again. It's as near as an actor will ever get to a regular nine-to-five job.

I wasn't that bothered any more about being type-cast; I'd had a year at *Coronation Street* and survived well enough. It was great. I'd been on television for many years before that, and I've never received the acclaim I got as Tosh for anything else I've played. It was quite extraordinary not being able to walk the streets uninterrupted any more.

I am one of the lucky ones in that recognition doesn't bother me. Awards, too, are just music to my ears. I love the praise, I have to admit it. Some of the best actors I know are very shy and in many ways, so am I.

I get asked to do after-dinner speaking all the time and I think I've done it twice, and hated it because it's not me. Or, to be more accurate, it is me, up there and exposed as I really am, rather than having a character and a script to hide myself behind. I was always quite shy, but I have learned how to get over it and not to let it show.

I can say a few words in public and get away with it, and afterwards people sometimes say it must be brilliant to be able to get up in front of thousands of people and look relaxed and confident. I can do it if I have to but, deep down, I find it nerve-racking.

The most confident people in the world don't make great actors. I think I was drawn to it in the first place to get over my lack of confidence. I had the craving, that need to be seen, to be good, and I suppose I am typical. I was a fatty at secondary school although I did well at sport, and I was certainly a fatty at junior school.

I have always felt overweight, which wasn't very pleasant when you knew that the big boys in the class could do things you couldn't. My way of hitting back, in typical Benny Hill fashion, was to be funny and make people laugh. They would say, 'Oh, Lloydy will do that', when it came to playing the fool. I used to get approval that way.

The part of Tosh in *The Bill* really was just tailor-made for me and I grabbed it with both hands. It felt like a hand-made suit of the highest class. I'm not saying it's easy to do, but I am saying it just felt right from the very start. I feel totally at one with Tosh. He has been very, very good to me and I hope I have been very good to him.

The police background that I had through my father, my uncle and my grandad meant that the role was there for me, and I was lucky enough to be given the chance.

I was delighted to get the part in a hit show. I'd already had chances of long-running television work in *Coronation Street* and in a comedy series called *Misfits*, written for me and Enn Reitel by Eric Chappell and Jean Warr. Eric had enjoyed enormous success with *Rising Damp*, and it looked as though we were on to a hit. It was our big break and Yorkshire TV were full of high hopes.

It was very successful but, unfortunately, it came out at the time of the ITV cutbacks. Despite reaching number five in the TV Top Ten, we were axed. It was all very disappointing.

Then *The Bill* came along so I was ready for some good news. I knew it was an important job and I knew it would change my life. I just didn't know at the time exactly how much.

When I started at our old place in Barlby Road, just off London's Ladbroke Grove, I did feel pretty nervous. It wasn't as daunting as my first day at *Coronation Street* because those faces were awesomely well known. They were like living legends.

But the stars of *The Bill* couldn't have been more welcoming. I knew Eric Richard who plays Sergeant Bob Cryer, and Larry Dann who used to play Sergeant

Alec Peters; they helped to introduce me around. I knew Eric because we had appeared in a film together. We both remember it because neither of us got paid for it. Then our paths crossed again when I appeared in the television production of Victoria Wood's play, *Talent.* I was sent to see the stage production of it at the ICA before we started work and Eric was playing the role of the slimy boyfriend that I had on TV. Eric was very kind and welcoming when I arrived. He is a sort of Dixon of Dock Green on *The Bill,* an experienced Sergeant who has been around and knows the ropes. He's just the sort of trusted, reliable copper you'd want to meet if you ever needed to call on the police in real life. He's something of an elder statesman in the show, a really good bloke.

In those days, we were all sharing two dressing-rooms, one for the men and one for the women. That meant about 16 blokes trying to grab a corner of the same room, which made life interesting. It was extraordinary.

At first, I was quite shocked by that, but there was real shortage of space there. Yet that wasn't important. We didn't mind that much because we could see that this wonderful series was coming together. All the energy and expertise seemed to gel together and as we relaunched the series in its new, snappier, half-hour format, I think we all began to realise that we were privileged to be in on the start of something big.

My first day filming *The Bill* was spent under the directorship of a very old friend of mine, Brian Farnham. I was working with a young actor called Jon Iles, whom I'd never met before.

Jon played DC Dashwood, and he is a very athletic young man, as I was soon to learn to my cost. The whole day was spent recording a chase after a young villain round a huge council estate. Jon is very tall and loped along with these huge strides and, although I was fitter then, my little legs had to move twice as fast as his to keep up.

I was absolutely exhausted when I got home that night, and it seemed as though every muscle in my body ached. I thought, 'I've never had a job like this before. I hope it doesn't carry on like this, because if it does, I won't last a week!'

Geoff McQueen is a great writer, but he was becoming so busy he was gradually becoming less involved. Tosh was the last character he devised and my first major episode was one of the last ones he ever wrote. It was called *Old-Fashioned Terms,* and it was a smashing story.

It involved the discovery of a young girl in a house, and there was a bit of a mystery about whether it was a drugs overdose. Tosh was suspicious and didn't think it was suicide.

There was an old man living downstairs, played by Trevor Peacock, and Tosh discovered that he'd been pestering her to sleep with him. Having been rejected, he murdered her. It was a terrific introduction to Tosh, because it established him straight away as an old-fashioned copper who operated much more by instinct than by the book.

Somehow, I seemed to get right into the character pretty quickly from the beginning. I dressed him with the help of the wardrobe bloke. Geoff had mapped out the idea of this scruffy guy in his late 30s who couldn't pay his mortgage. I already had short hair because I was playing an army Sergeant in *The Foreigner.* And I was clean shaven.

But the producers had Geoff's idea of 'scruffy copper' firmly in their minds, so they asked me when I got the part if I would be prepared to put on some weight. I was only 12st 4lb at the time, but I found putting the weight on remarkably easy. And eating on the job became part of Tosh's character. I always seemed to be scoffing something.

We did one scene in which my car was going through a car wash and I was eating a Mars bar. We did ten takes, so I got through ten bars in one morning, which is a lot of calories.

They asked me to grow my hair and I suggested a moustache and sideburns. They said, 'Great, do that.' The moustache was so important in the early days of establishing Tosh that on my first publicity photos, I wore a false one because my own hadn't quite grown through.

I was just finishing filming a Thames TV series called *Young Charlie Chaplin*, in which I played Fred Karno, the clean-shaven bloke who found Chaplin. Once the filming had finished, I started growing my own moustache underneath the false one, which was a very unpleasant experience.

I chose the famous macintosh and it has become a vital part of Tosh's character. I knew there were echoes of *Columbo* at the start, but it has really worked well for me. If I'm not wearing one, everyone asks me where my mac is.

Over the nine years I have been playing Tosh, I have refused all attempts to get me to wear a new mac. It's falling to bits and it has to be continually patched up, but I love it and won't change it. It has become a good-luck symbol for me after all this time. I'm determined to keep it right to the end and then ... who knows ..?

auction it for thousands of pounds? We also worked out that Tosh would only ever have one suit because he couldn't afford another one. They put me in a navy-blue suit and I think I now have about four or five, all exactly the same. I must be the most under-dressed bloke on television.

I also have a deeply dull selection of really bland shirts, all either blue or cream. Tosh only ever wears boring shirts and he has a weird assortment of ties, mostly really naff! He just doesn't care about clothes and certainly couldn't be accused of being a fashion icon.

He just gets out of bed and slings on the first thing that's handy, because he's always late for work. I remember when I dressed as Tosh for the first time, it was when I slipped on the heavy-duty shoes that I began to feel like a copper. I always wear trainers or light shoes, so Tosh's big, black, heavy clodhoppers just made me feel different, as though I had joined up for real.

Dressing as Tosh has always been very important to me. Right from the start, as the clothes went on I gradually felt Tosh come to life.

Viewers of *The Bill* have found out more about Tosh Lines than just about any other character in the series. We see them all in action at work, but we don't see much of their home lives. Yet viewers have seen Tosh's wife, played by Lesley Duff, and his children, played by three of my own kids.

Lesley is quite an attractive lady, but as Tosh's wife she is dressed to look fairly dowdy. She has actually been back in *The Bill* since then and has played a glamorous prostitute and other roles. I think only Tosh, Sergeant Cryer (who had a son appear in an episode)

f Wiedersehen, Pet! As Harry Blackburn, 1984-85.

Above: Squeeze that teat! I was playing Simple Simon in *Dick Whittington*.

Opposite: I've always loved doing panto. As Buttons in *Cinderella*, Bristol Old Vic, 1981.

Barbara Windsor was touring the country with an old time music hall, so I just had to giv her a leg-up!

ith Malandra Burrows at Birmingham Hippodrome.

My wedding day.

op: Left to right: My mum, my mother in law, cousin Sally and Auntie Pauline.

ottom: At our wedding with young Mark (left) and Sophie.

With little Elly on the beach just across from Burgh Island near Salcombe.

p: James watching his mum and dad relaxing in the sea.

ttom: The caravan at Salcome beach, cricketing with (left to right) Poppy, James, Elly, *nry* and Edward.

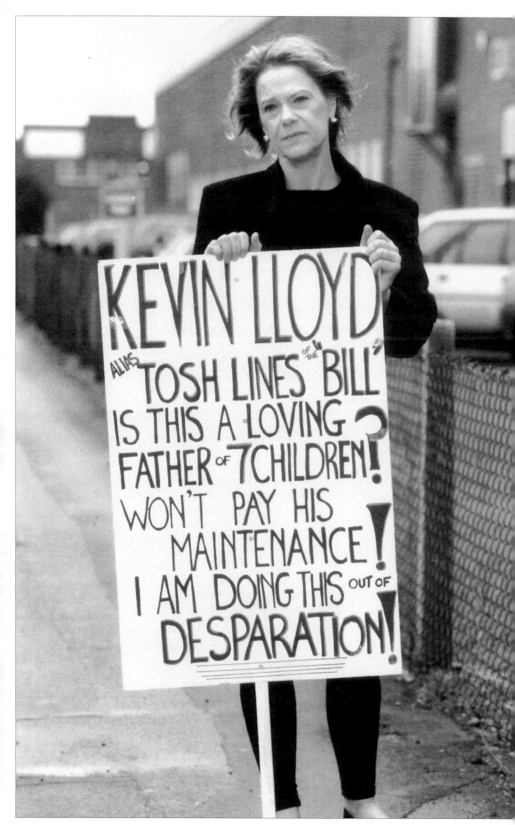

Lesley's protest outside the studios. It just made me sad.

p: At Derby Playhouse with Brian Clough. He was a hero who became a friend.

ottom: Su Pollard and Ray Meagher came to help open our delicatessen in Duffield.

Top: Robert Maxwell added my favourite football club to his long list of possessions, but the fans never took to him.

Bottom: Meeting Princess Anne after the panto at Birmingham Hippodrome was a proud moment.

p: Tosh in animated action with a corpse.

ttom: The boys and girls from *The Bill*.

Top: We won the National Television Award for best drama serial, and I got to kiss Fergie who presented it.

Bottom: On the set of *The Bill* when my kids played Tosh's kids in an episode called *Don't like Mondays*. James, Poppy and Henry played James, Poppy and Henry.

sh, with his most lived in look.

With Rita, the lady who lifted me up when I was really down. She's a gem.

and Trudie Goodwin's character (who had a couple of boyfriends), have given a glimpse of life beyond Sun Hill.

My very first entrance to Sun Hill was Tosh arriving late through the gates on foot. In the early days, Tosh travelled everywhere by bus because he was too hard up to buy a car but, eventually, he got a beaten-up old Volvo estate.

That made me feel even more at home with the character because that's exactly what the family car was at the time. They were even both the same colour — silver. In the programme, it was always breaking down or refusing to start. That led to some funny moments when I arrived for a big investigation on the bus. Tosh isn't too good with transport.

Originally, I was supposed to make my first entrance carrying a briefcase, but I changed that to a carrier bag because I thought it would suit Tosh better. The new detective certainly looked different from most of the other clean-cut and bright-eyed young recruits. But it seemed to work a treat.

The boss at *The Bill* then was a guy called Lloyd Shirley, a legendary drama producer who had been behind shows like *The Sweeney*, and apparently he was delighted by scruffy Tosh. I got a big thumbs up from him and I've never looked back. He said, 'This is the character we've been looking for since we started.' He went completely overboard about the character. It was fortunate for me because the viewers seemed to like Tosh as well.

I remember after that first appearance in *Old-Fashioned Terms*, Mark Wingett (who plays Carver and has become a close friend) and I were filming in the street with cars hooting as they passed and drivers shouting, 'Hey-up, Tosh!' The programme had only gone out a night or two before. The recognition was very quick indeed.

The writers are very clever, often making the most of those little character features. I really enjoyed an episode written by PJ Hammond called *Black Monday*. Tosh's ancient Volvo had broken down yet again on the way to work, so he got on the bus and saw someone who was supposed to have committed suicide years ago when he was nicked for a banking fraud on Tosh's previous patch in Essex. The lads back at the office thought he was cracking up, and couldn't understand why he was bothering to rake up the past.

But, of course, tenacious Tosh wasn't cracking up at all. He simply had the bit between his teeth and he wouldn't let go — and it turns out he's absolutely right. The man had reappeared in the Sun Hill area as the chief accountant in a building society and was offending again. It was a smashing story and it summed up Tosh perfectly.

In our business, if you are lucky once in a while, a part comes along that suits you to a T. There's an awful lot of me in Tosh and I suppose now there's even quite a bit of Tosh in me. I like to think he's a good bloke. Tosh has been wonderfully good for me and I hope that Kevin Lloyd hasn't been too bad for him.

I am sure if I had followed my father's example and become a copper for real, I would have been a lot like Tosh. I'd have been told off loads of times for arriving late and I certainly wouldn't be a fast-track promotion chaser. Viewers often think that it's high time for Tosh to be promoted, but the drawback is that if that happened, police procedure would require him to move. So he's turned down promotion opportunities three times, including one posting to Ireland.

He passed his Sergeant's exams which is great for Tosh, but I don't think he wants the responsibility and he doesn't want anything to get in the way of him spending time with his wife and kids.

And I certainly don't want to leave the show. Real coppers come up to me all the time and tell me they like Tosh, and they especially admire his ability to wrap up a case in 25 minutes with a minimum of paperwork. That's television for you!

I love Tosh. I think you have to find something you love about any character you play, and with Tosh it's not difficult. He stands up for what is right and he is a very lovable character and great fun to play. We are a very close-knit team and generally very good friends. What you see on the screen is usually the tense, serious side, but between takes we're inclined to have a few laughs. And in some cases, more than a few. Sometimes, messing about is the only way to remain sane.

There was a sort of 'initiation test' early on that went down in *The Bill* history. It involved a scene between me, Chris Ellison as Burnside and Peter Ellis as Brownlow.

Peter and I are very good friends. It was in the TV version of *Talent* that our friendship started, long before he became one of my bosses in *The Bill*. Brownlow looks down on Tosh because he's scruffy, late and disorganised, everything he hates about the police.

We were talking about this case of mine and I had to say a line that went something like, 'I had another case like that once, sir. I remember it well. It involved a man called Randolph Tangles.' And this ridiculous name that Geoff McQueen had made up had us in complete fits.

Have you ever in your wildest dreams heard of a man called Randolph Tangles? We just couldn't do it. These were my very early days and I was still trying to make a good impression, but I couldn't speak. They had to say, 'Who?' and then I had to say 'Randolph Tangles' again. It just wasn't humanly possible, particularly not with us three. Peter Ellis might look very sombre and superior on screen, but in real life he is one of the worst gigglers I've known.

That day, we went to 22 takes, never getting any further than 'Randolph Tangles'. In the end, the three of us were crying, and we had to get through it by staring at the floor as we spoke. Sometimes you can pull yourself together, but that day we had gone way past that point.

And when we finally did get through it, the cameraman cracked up so we still had to do it again. Laughter is very infectious. Three hours later, it was over. But I still have that episode on tape and you can see we've all been laughing. I've been convinced to this day that it was some form of initiation test.

Peter Ellis and I joke sometimes that we never meet. I've been in *The Bill* for nine years now and I think we've only ever met each other on screen three times. Maybe they are trying to keep us apart after the Randolph Tangles incident.

We do three a week and sometimes we even do four if they are trying to find time in the schedule for doing more of the popular hour-long specials. The workload has increased but fortunately so has the staff to cope with it. In the early days, we seemed to be working all the time. There are three separate production units running all the time, colour-coded red, blue and green for different episodes. Each one takes any five days out of seven to record.

There is no overtime if you have to work on a weekend. Each production team has its own producer, director and lighting and camera teams. The actors move around from week to week depending on which story their character is involved in. But sometimes they even have to move around from day to day, and I still hold the record for changing between different episodes five times in one day. That was pretty hair-raising. It is all run like a military operation. Sometimes it gets a bit difficult, but you just have to cope with it.

Since we moved to our new headquarters at Merton, we have much more space for everyone and more dressing-rooms. We each share with one other person. Andy McIntosh and I have dressing-room 4, and get on well together. The Merton base is situated within an industrial estate, and contains our purpose-built Sun Hill set, with a huge warehouse covering all the nick, the cells, a magistrate's court and a hospital. All the casting people are there, and we have our own and the Sun Hill canteen.

There is talk of a pub being built as well, but that hasn't happened yet. The complex is called Bosun House, named after Bosun the dog owned by our Executive Producer, Michael Chapman. There's even a photo of the dog at the gates.

We all tease each other. You have to in a hard-working team. It's our way of helping each other to relieve the tension and the pressure. When we had Letitia Dean from *Eastenders* starring as a woman at the centre of an arson investigation, she was in hysterics at the clowning. I often rehearse as Tommy Cooper, one of my heroes. It's just something I do, but if you don't have any advanced warning, I suppose it can be a shade surprising. I did have one rookie director years ago become quite upset. It was during a scene with Chris Ellison, and afterwards the director came up to me all flustered and said, 'You're not actually going to do it like that, are you?'

I played it serious and said, 'Well, yes. That's my character. That's Tosh.'

'But it sounds like Tommy Cooper,' said the poor bloke, and then Ellison and I cracked up laughing.

Sometimes, I wonder why the out-takes don't end up on *It'll Be Alright on the Night* more often. I did a wonderful one with Russell Boulter who plays DS Boulton. We were supposed to jump in the car and rush off after someone, but each time we did it he put the car in reverse and we shot off backwards. I find it very hard to stop giggling after something like that.

The trouble is that if you're a giggler, there will always be something around to spark you off. One famous burst of hysterics was caused by a door. There was a scene with Chris Ellison, Tony Scannell, Tom Cotcher and myself in which we had to break down a door, run into a house and drag out a gang of villains. They were particularly huge baddies, and would have had no problem beating us up in real life. One was played by Danny McAlinden, the ex-boxer.

I had to smash the door in with one of those police sledge-hammers, but after the first couple of blows the door refused to budge.

The third time, I missed the door and hit the frame, taking a chunk out of it. Everyone was mumbling, 'Come on Lloydy, for goodness sake, knock it down.'

But by then, unfortunately, we got the giggles. Luckily, the camera was filming us from behind so no one could see us laughing. I wielded the sledge-hammer for a fourth time, and finally the door caved in. Burnside yelled, 'Come on,' and we all made for the entrance.

It didn't help that Tom Cotcher was always a rather awkward guy, and he managed to trip over the doorstep. Like something out of the Keystone Cops, we all fell on top of him in a great, giggling heap. Danny McAlinden and all his henchmen looked very surprised.

After that, getting anything vaguely sensible out of us was difficult to say the least. The door was wrecked so we had to wait an hour for a carpenter to knock up another one, but we were laughing for longer than that.

There is an awful lot of teasing each other. Often, if you have to pass a message to someone, you'll look down and see a note that reads: 'Get your lines right this time.' And if anyone has to open a filing cabinet or a desk drawer in a scene, he will occasionally find something that certainly shouldn't be there. Tony Scannell was always an interesting chap to work with. He's the only man I know who has ever dropped of to sleep during a scene.

We were supposed to be driving off in the police car with me at the wheel talking to him in the passenger seat. But I think he had enjoyed a long night out the previous evening, and when we got to the take I drove off with the cameras rolling and I had to say, 'What do you think, Sergeant?' But instead of a reply, I got snoring. Tony was fast asleep.

He managed to fall asleep again in the back of the car

while filming with Chris Ellison. There was a memorable shot of him sliding down the window.

In the early days, CID was great and could have carried a series on its own. Chris Ellison was terrific as Burnside, Tony Scannell, despite his peculiar behaviour, was often excellent as Roach, and with Andy McIntosh, Jon Iles, Nula Conwell and Mark Wingett, I felt I was in really great company. We all had good, strong, well-defined characters, and we got on like a house on fire.

I've made some great friends. And it has gone from strength to strength since then. Shaun Scott, who plays Deakin, has got a lovely sense of humour. He's the danger man for making you laugh. In one scene, he was supposed to say to me, 'What are you going to do, Tosh, if your radio goes on the blink?' But like all of us sometimes, his mind wasn't quite linked to his mouth and it came out: 'What are you going to do, Tosh, if your radio goes on the blonk?' It doesn't sound much, but that's all you need for a burst of hysterics. He had to go outside and have a cigarette to calm down. They sent me out to him, me of all people, to have a chat to try to help him stop corpsing.

I have so many memories of being unable to control my laughter. There was a time when Tosh had to break the news to some parents that their son had died. John Forgeham was playing the father, and it was a very sad little scene in the CID office. Tosh had to explain that the lad had died and that there would have to be a post mortem.

When we got to it, naturally everyone was silent. You could have heard a pin drop as I said, 'I'm afraid there will have to be a porst motem.'

It took about another five seconds of complete silence

for exactly what I said to dawn on everyone. They all then cracked up laughing.

At first, I couldn't understand what the joke was until they played it back to me. Of course, when we started to re-shoot the scene, I just couldn't get the line right. I did everything I could to concentrate. I went to the toilet and tried to pull myself together. The cameraman, my dear friend Rolie Luka, was laughing so much he had to get the cameraman to fix the camera on automatic to get the scene. He just said, 'Don't move,' and left the studio. He couldn't stand it any more.

It took so long to get it right that one of the crew took a photograph and had it framed and presented it to me in the pub one lunchtime.

We work at great speed and much of the dialogue and action, because this is a police series, is very, very serious. So your natural reaction, if you've got a sense of humour like mine, is to laugh whenever you know that you can't. It's our escape.

What makes *The Bill* so special to me is the camaraderie between the actors and the crew. We really get on extremely well. It is a tremendously professional outfit because whenever it comes to helping each other out, we are always there for each other. I've made some very good friends. Lines and Carver often work together which is great, because Mark Wingett and I have become good pals.

We once had to arrest a huge guy which turned into a frightening experience. With some actors, the word 'Action' has an alarming effect. They have a tendency to pull all the stops out, which is OK if it's a dialogue scene, but if it's a fight then you'd better watch out. Carver and Lines had rehearsed and rehearsed with this chap, but things turned out quite differently when we started the scene for real. We heard the word 'Action', and this animal appeared from nowhere. He did everything at ten times the speed, and we still had to grab him, throw him on the bed and Carver had to cuff him. The bloke went mad and a real fight ensued, with arms and elbows flying everywhere.

The guy was fighting for his freedom, and certainly didn't want to be handcuffed. It was as if no one had told him the plot, or if they had, he had evidently forgotten it. Thankfully, Mark is quite fit and strong and I wasn't in such bad shape, so after a frantic minute or two we got him under control — we had to leap on top of him, put our knees in his back and force him into the handcuffs.

Eventually, when we dragged him to his feet to bundle him into the car and take him back to Sun Hill, we found that we had made an important mistake. In the scuffle, Carver hadn't handcuffed himself to the madman but to me! We didn't find out until we got up and this character realised he was still free. He was left lying on the bed perfectly able to get up and run away.

We had another unfortunate experience where a villain was just supposed to run through a door, down some stairs and away from us. We rehearsed this carefully beforehand, but when we went for it he was like a tornado. He dived at us, ran all over us and rushed down the stairs. He was supposed to get away, but he didn't want to leave without bashing us up first. It was horrendous.

We do try to do our own stunts wherever possible. Mark loves it and so do I, but I'm not quite as fit as I used to be and I'm a bit older now. Mark talked me into one particular stunt, though, where we were supposed to be turned over in a car. We were supposed to arrest a guy, sparking a load of trouble. The result is a rampaging hoard of Pakistanis after us, who eventually trap us in our police car and turn it upside down with Carver and Lines inside it. They asked me if I would do it and I thought it sounded dangerous. Of course, Mark and I soon decided to have a go. And as it turned out, we had to do it twice to get enough shots.

We were securely strapped in with special seat-belts. They said the roof wouldn't cave in, and we would just be left dangling upside-down, but perfectly safe. They'd then quickly come and get us out. I wasn't too keen on it, but when we came to do it, the scenes did look fantastic. It was pretty frightening, first being rocked in a car and then being turned over, hanging there suspended in space. In the commotion, Mark managed to put his foot through the windscreen so there was glass everywhere and, because of the positions we were in, I was left hanging upside-down for about 25 minutes, which wasn't very pleasant.

In fact, when an American producer saw it later, he asked how on earth they had got two stuntmen who looked so much like the actors. He couldn't believe that actors had done it. In America, the insurance people would never have allowed it, and the actors just wouldn't do it.

I've done quite a few things on *The Bill* which have felt dangerous. I've rolled downstairs in a fight which might not sound too spectacular, but you try doing it without suffering a few bruises. I couldn't. One of the worst bumps I've had was in a big raid we did in an underground car park. We had all been in hiding, waiting for the suspect, and when the order came through to grab him we all rushed in. Unfortunately for me, one of my colleagues jumped out of his car, and I ran straight into the open car door. I was sent flying. The bruises that day went purple.

The people from *The Bill* were fantastic when I was going through the problems with my marriage. They were tremendously supportive, particularly our boss, Michael Chapman. In truth, everyone has been very kind and helpful. I was very lucky I was working on *The Bill* when everything blew up. Other casts and production teams might not have been quite so understanding. When your wife is standing outside the building with a placard, it hits you really hard. You're hurt, embarrassed and upset. But you've still got to carry on working. We work very long hours and, for once, I was grateful for that. Work was a great thing to throw myself into at the time. Without it, I'm sure I would have gone under.

It's a very friendly, sociable show. We mostly enjoy each other's company off screen as well as on. We don't live in each other's pockets, but we have some good times together. We've got our own football and cricket teams.

Work starts early, at 7.00am most days, so I have taken to staying down in London much more than I did, because the first train from Derby doesn't get in until after 7.00am. I stay in a little hotel near the studios. By the time you have finished a day's filming, all you are good for is a quick drink in the pub and then back to the hotel to learn my lines for the next day.

There are lots of reasons for the success of *The Bill*, particularly the fact that many different factors came right at the right time: the quality of the writing, casting and production values is tremendous. Only the very best standards are accepted. The executive producer, Michael Chapman, leads from the front. He was in charge when *The Bill* started off with the hour-long pilot *Woodentop*, and although he retires in 1997, he still drives the whole team as hard and as enthusiastically as ever.

It's very unusual for an actor to have a job that lasts a year, let alone nine. I wouldn't have stayed with *The Bill* unless I had really enjoyed just about every minute. Before *The Bill* I was always lucky enough to stay in work, but I was flitting from one job to another all the time like many other actors. It's the excitement and uncertainty that brings people into the business, but *The Bill* has changed that for me and for loads of other people. It's an exceptional job in an extraordinary profession. I am totally committed to the show and I think all the other actors are as well. There's such a great spirit between us that every time we get a script we go all out to do the best possible job. We all put a lot into it and hopefully it comes over on the screen. It really is a team.

The writers, the technical people, the actors, make-up, wardrobe, design, everyone is fighting for the same thing to make the shows as good as they can possibly be. We don't carry any passengers. It's a very tight ship. There are no stars in *The Bill*. Sun Hill is the star.

Lesley took it very well when I became a household name. She has always accepted me becoming public property very well. It couldn't have been easy for her. I know she never particularly liked being introduced as Mrs Kevin Lloyd when she is a very high-powered businesswoman in her own right. But she would always be at my side and she used to advise me on how I should handle things. She would always be there for me.

For years, it was fine for me to be living in Duffield and commuting down to London to be Tosh. It was particularly good for Abbey Taxis, who used to take me backwards and forwards to the station. I think I must have bought a cab or two over the years. And very good for British Rail. I think I've been one of their biggest fund-raisers.

I always came home at night because I wanted to kiss the kids goodnight and sleep in my own bed. I didn't want my children to think that daddy lived anywhere but at home. I liked them to know that daddy was coming home. Many, many times I arrived home very late and then got up before the crack of dawn to get the 5.05am train back to London. It might sound ridiculous to some people, but that was what I wanted. I did not want to sleep on my own in an anonymous flat or hotel room. I wanted to sleep in my own bed with my wife and my kids in the house.

It mattered very much to me that I was actually at home. Even if they did not know I had kissed them goodnight, it still meant a lot to me. The alternative was the family having to move back to London. There was no choice, really, once the children had settled in well at Ecclesbourne. It was better that I suffered occasionally, rather than Lesley and the kids. Of course, looking back, I should have stayed over a lot more, I can see that now, and perhaps avoided becoming so knackered. My diabetes came from somewhere, and the doctors said it was partly brought on by stress.

And if you think I like a drink, you ought to try a night out with Tony Scannell. Tony and I go back a long way. He's a little older than me but he was still a year behind me at drama school.

148

After Roach and Tosh Lines were both well established, Tony and I were asked over to Belfast to appear on a popular chat show, the *Gerry Kelly Show*, to talk about the programme. Tony will probably hate me for reminding him of his antics, but I think he hates me anyway, so that's fine. The show goes out live at 11.00pm. I flew out after I finished filming at teatime and I arrived at the Belfast studios in the evening.

Gerry said, 'Hello, Kevin, pleased to meet you. Where's Mr Scannell?'

I didn't know, I hadn't seen him — he'd flown in on the plane before mine. Michael Fish, the weather forecaster, was also on the show, and he chipped in that he'd been on the plane with Tony and quietly suggested, 'I think you had better look in the pubs of Belfast for Mr Scannell.'

It seemed that Tony had had a drink and then set out from the airport apparently in urgent search of another one. The last Michael Fish had seen of him, Tony was on the brandy.

Gerry Kelly went pale and said, 'Oh my God! What are we going to do?'

I felt embarrassed because we were both in the same show, and although it was nothing to do with me, I felt responsible. They sent out runners to scour the bars for Tony. I was there with my brother Terry. As 11.00pm approached, the mood in the studio became steadily more tense. With an hour to go, Gerry Kelly came up to me and said, 'Kev, me old darling, sorry to put this on you but will you do the whole interview on your own?'

This meant talking for 45 minutes, which is a long time to fill, unless you happen to be Peter Ustinov. But I said, 'I'll have to. I'll do my best.'

'Great,' said Gerry with understandable relief,

because there was still no sign of Scannell.

Then just half-an-hour before the show, Scannell arrived. He was happy as a parrott and twice as talkative. Nervous young assistants started ferrying him black coffee.

Before you could say, 'Get me out of here,' it was time to do the show. So we moved into the wings of the set and Gerry started with the introductions. We were standing there waiting to appear live in front of three million people and Scannell squared up to me and said with surprising clarity, 'You've never f****** liked me, have you?'

I turned to him and replied, 'Now is not the time, Tony. We'll talk about it afterwards. I suggest you try to get yourself sober and we'll go on and try to do the show.'

I was terrified at the prospect of doing a 45-minute interview all on my own with the help of Scannell sitting next to me. I wondered what on earth he was going to come out with. But then Gerry got to the end of his introductions.

' ...and a big Irish welcome to Kevin Lloyd and Tony Scannell from *The Bill* ...' and we tried to switch on the smiles and walked out to face the cameras.

I was aware that Tony in this state was like an accident waiting to happen. Gerry concentrated completely on me, asking all about the family. Scannell kept leaning across and saying something like, 'Hello, I'm here as well, you know,' which was unnerving to say the least. This went on for ages.

But as the end of the first half approached, Gerry felt he couldn't totally exclude Scannell. So he looked over and said, 'Ah well, Tony, coming to you now. You are an Irishman yourself, you were born and bred here.

Where were you born?'

'Ah,' drawled Tony, almost falling out of his chair, 'I was born near the coast.'

I wondered what was coming next.

'I was born in a little town called Muff.'

I thought, 'Oh no, he can't possibly ...'

Then he added, '... a little town called Muff and there is a lot of diving goes on down there. They call them Muff Divers,' and he grinned wickedly.

There was a complete silence from the audience and suddenly the camera flashed back to me and a flushed-looking Gerry who asked me, 'And how old is your oldest child, Kevin?'

It was quite an experience. I said '19' and we were off again. I tried to continue while thinking that I couldn't believe what he had just said. I tried to focus on the family and, right at the end, Scannell leaned across and shouted, 'I'm still here, you know. Why don't you talk to me again?'

At the end, when the lights finally came down and the show was mercifully over, Gerry Kelly said very quietly to a glazed Scannell, 'I didn't like that muff-diving joke at all.' The evening was beautifully rounded off by a fight with the cameraman and the director at a party afterwards at the Europa Hotel.

Sadly, Tony's troubles in Belfast didn't even end there. Next morning, I woke up to find that my car had arrived, with the driver saying, 'It was a good show last night. Your friend is a bit of a lad. He is still in the Belfast General Hospital.' Apparently, someone had thumped him in a bar.

Tony was right about one thing though — I never did particularly like him, and I'm sure the feeling was mutual. He was an arrogant man, but he was also a very fine actor. I don't think he ever got over carrying a spear to my *Macbeth* and, when we met up again on *The Bill*, we were never mates.

I always admire distinctive characters. I even quite liked Robert Maxwell, that unorthodox multi-millionaire who once decided to add my football team to his long list of playthings. Fortunately, I never had the misfortune to work for him, or to let him get his hands on my pension. But I did warm to him when he came to the Baseball Ground, which was more than most of the fans did. They were chanting 'F*** off, Maxwell'. I was sitting behind him and I was hit on the back of the head by a rolled up programme that I assumed was aimed at Captain Bob. But the abuse didn't bother him. He was a bit deaf and he didn't catch what they were saying. He just heard his name and waved genially back. It was only at half-time when some of the Arsenal directors sympathised and told him how disgraceful it was that he should have to put up with that sort of language, that he realised just what people thought of him.

Fame can be very intoxicating and my most heady flirtation with it was when Michael Aspel surprised me with his legendary big red book for my appearance on *This Is Your Life*. People sometimes say they take it in their stride, but not me. The whole experience really knocked me sideways. It was back in 1992, but I can recall it as though it were yesterday. I had already appeared as a guest on Alan Bleasdale's *This Is Your Life*, along with Pete Postlethwaite, Matthew Kelly and Julie Waters, because of our days in *Scully*.

The penny never dropped, even when the researchers began chatting away to me after the show. I never twigged. I just thought that for some reason, they found me fascinating company. They started by asking me all sorts of questions about my past to see if they could put a programme together. They even asked me how I would react if I was the subject of the show, and I just said, 'Ooh, Crikey, it's been great for Alan Bleasdale ... it would be an enormous honour.'

The day they actually sprang it on me was very weird. I wasn't supposed to be filming after the first scene of the day. Then I was off and I was all set to jump on the train home. I thought I would be finished by 10.00 am. But things are planned to the last detail. I got a phonecall from our director saying, 'Kev, you're not going to like this, I'm sorry. We have got to do this night shot from another episode, so we will have to wait until it gets dark.' I was really fed up at having to hang around for a whole day between two tiny shots.

They had even written a fictitious scene for me, which involved driving round to the front of *The Bill* set which had to be in the dark. So I left home on the 5.00 am train that morning, little realising that when I kissed the kids goodbye, all the older ones were already fully dressed underneath the bedclothes and ready for the journey themselves. They were going to be on the next train down to London after mine, to do some filming to be used in the show. The younger ones weren't dressed because Lesley didn't think she could rely on them to keep a secret. But James, Poppy and Henry were all dressed and ready to go. They were filmed in police uniforms doing the famous walk from *The Bill*.

So when I got to London and rang Lesley up, like I always did, there was no reply, which baffled me. I did my first scene and then sat down for my nine-hour wait. And became grumpier and grumpier as the day dragged on. I rang Lesley again. No reply, and I became even more irritated. Then I rang my old friend, Arthur Titterton, just to have a chat about football I think, only to be told that he had gone to London for some big court case. Well, I had seen Arthur a day or so before, and he hadn't mentioned anything to me about it. I rang another mate, Patrick O'Connor, the editor of the local paper for which I used to write my weekly column, only to be told, 'Sorry, Kevin, he has had to go to London for a few days for a major awards ceremony.' My irritation grew and I became very curious as to why my friends were coming down to London without telling me. I had been with Patrick the day before handing in my copy, and he had never said anything about going to London.

But I thought no more of it. It was obviously just a very strange day. Wherever I went, people left. I cleared rooms effortlessly and I began to think I had developed a body odour problem. I realised later that they were terrified of blurting out the big secret. Even Michael Chapman, the boss of *The Bill*, walked in at one point, saw me and said 'Oh', and walked quickly out again. I thought, 'Crikey. What have I done?' I went down to the pub at lunchtime and had a couple of drinks with Mike Purcell, when he suddenly said, 'Let's go to another pub.' I refused and he started behaving very oddly. I only found out later that he had been sent out to mind me, and he was trying to get me out of harm's way.

I was getting more and more rattled about having to hang about, and I said to the director quite firmly, 'Look, I must be on the 8.00 pm train to Derby because I am off work tomorrow. I'm not mucking about.' It got to about 6.00 pm and, as it was February, it was absolutely pitch black. When I asked whether we could start filming, they said it wasn't dark enough. I couldn't believe it. It seemed like the world was conspiring against me. I sat fuming in my dressing-room but they kept putting me off until Aspel arrived. They even said the camera had broken down, which happens occasionally, and I swallowed that.

When we came to do the scene with me driving round and picking up WPC Kathy Marshall (played by Lynn Millar), the director came up to me beforehand and said, 'Whatever happens, Kev, just keep going. Just ad-lib because we haven't got time for another take and if we don't get it in this one we'll have to come back tomorrow to do it.' So, eventually, I got into the police car, they shouted action, I drove round and got out to pick up the WPC. Just as I called out to her, all hell was let loose — screeching tyres, flashing lights and cars arrived from all over the place. I almost panicked. I didn't know what on earth was going on. But I had in the back of my mind the director's instruction to keep going whatever happened. I genuinely thought, 'Crikey. There must have been more pages in the script than I thought. I must have missed something.' Anyway, a car screeched to a halt just missing me. Burnside and Carver, Chris Ellison and Mark Wingett, got out. Graham Cole who plays Stamp had been driving. Chris said, 'Quick, Tosh, there is somebody very important to see you.' I thought to myself, 'I don't know my lines but I must keep going.' I jumped back in the car but Chris got me out and I just remember this big red thing coming towards me and all these lights flashing...

The whole place lit up and I could see people appearing from behind bushes and cars and buildings where they had been hiding, and at last I realised it was Michael Aspel and his big red book. The first thing that crossed my mind was, 'Gosh. Who is he doing?' I looked round and there was nobody there but me. Then Michael came up and said the famous *This Is Your Life* words to me. I went as white as a sheet and thought I was going to have a heart-attack. It was an extraordinary moment, I'll never forget it. It was one of the best nights of my life.

Full credit to Lesley, she did a great job helping the researchers. She was under a lot of pressure, especially during the last two weeks when quite a lot of people have to be let in on the secret. She did nearly give it away once. The main researcher on my programme was Mandy Nixon, David Nixon's daughter, and Lesley nearly said to me once, 'Guess who I met today ... Mandy Nixon.' But she stopped herself just in time.

I did have that strange experience of several unexplained phonecalls. Lesley had another shop then and the phone there always seemed to be engaged. Whenever I walked in, she would be on the phone and then quickly say 'Goodbye' and hang up. That happened quite a few times and I thought she was behaving very oddly, but it never even occurred to me that she might have been having an affair. I know that when Ronnie Barker had it done to him he was convinced that his wife was having an affair, and I can understand that. Things weren't right but I couldn't put my finger on it. Lesley just seemed so nervy and on tenterhooks all the time that I went to our GP and asked about Lesley and tried to fix an appointment. She just went to the doctor and explained the problem.

The show went so well. I was terribly nervous because before you go on, you're settled into a luxurious trailer which they use as a waiting room, so that you can't see people arriving. I was offered champagne and lobster and plenty of wonderful food but I was in the dark about what was going on and feeling pretty uneasy about going on television without having learned my script. I felt like a condemned man in his cell waiting for the executioner. Fortunately, I knew the make-up girl and she calmed me down a little. I was desperately concerned that I hadn't got a suit but, of course, Lesley had taken care of all that as well.

Michael Aspel was fantastic. He couldn't have been nicer. I remember being in the wings with him. He said, 'Are you nervous?'

I said, 'Nervous? I'm terrified. I would much rather have a five page speech in *The Bill* than do this, not knowing what is going to happen.'

'Kev,' he said, 'I get as nervous as that every time I do it.'

And that made me feel so much better. When the show started, the wonderful warmth of the whole occasion just bowled me over. I have to hand it to Lesley, she played a blinder organising that.

CHAPTER NINE

ELLY

Our children are all very different. Mark is 25 now and very career minded. He is doing extremely well as a photographer and has been working very successfully in New York.

Sophie is working for Lonsdale Travel in Derby, but I don't think she quite knows what she wants to do.

James is 18 now and, like Henry who is 15, has suffered from dyslexia. Henry has a more serious condition, but he has the strength of character and sense of humour to get over it. James is a bit more introverted and finds it more of a hurdle to cope with, but that is why I was so delighted to read in the paper that he is going to go to university. It was just such a shame that that was how I had to hear such good news.

I am very proud of them both.

Poppy is 16 now and she is a wonderfully sweet and pretty girl. She and Henry look like me I think, except fortunately they're not quite so ugly. James and Poppy scrap all the time and, with Henry, we always call them the triplets because they are so close together in age. We had three children in not much more than three years. I don't think I slept a wink for three years, and neither did Lesley.

Lesley did become pregnant again about six years ago, but sadly she lost the baby. That was very traumatic for both of us. He was not planned but the loss of a baby is worse than anything else. It was very difficult to get over, but the baby wasn't well. It wasn't forming properly inside the womb and she miscarried half-way through her pregnancy. Lesley had already decided he was to be called Kevin, so I felt a special sadness. I was in the West End doing a play and I was trying to get back to her at the Nuffield when she christened him Kevin. It was awful when he died. I thought at the time that nobody in the world should be put through this, but losing both Chloe and now Kevin was something we had to live with. Divorce is also something that no one should be put through.

After that, Lesley really threw herself into charity work. She became involved with a Derby-based charity called Treats, which aimed to deliver aid to innocent victims of war-torn Romania. It was run by a lady called Josie Webb, the wife of my old friend Stuart Webb, one of the leading lights at Derby County. The revolution in Romania and the overthrow of Ceaucescu had brought to international attention the many young victims of that evil régime, and Treats was working in conjunction with the *Derby Evening Telegraph* to try to help them. We had seen some of the horror stories on the news and I knew Lesley to be very interested, so I suggested she get in touch with Josie to see if she could help in any way. It all started from there.

Lesley became a member of Treats initially, and became so involved that she subsequently ended up as Chairman. One fundraising event was held in a lovely old country house, at which Victoria Wood had generously agreed to perform her act. She was terrific. Many friends supported us that night, including June Brown and some pals from *The Bill* — Trudie Goodwin, Ben Roberts and Peter Ellis — and we raised nearly £10,000.

Lesley went out to Romania twice with Treats delivering all sorts of aid. When she came back the second time, I could see that she was even more upset than she had been by her first visit. She was devastated. Seeing young children in orphanages is desperately upsetting, particularly if you love children as much as Lesley. She came back very moved. Her attitude was one of compassion, quite rightly, because she's a lovely, caring, lady.

She sat me down and asked me if there was any chance that we could adopt a Romanian baby. She just felt that we had so much over here and they had nothing. There was room in our house for another child and she just wanted to help in any way that she could. My immediate reaction was to say, 'Yes'. And, in all honesty, I had already known from the start that as soon as Lesley became seriously involved, it would end up with us adopting a Romanian baby. I just knew it would.

The day Lesley flew out to Romania for the first time was the day Little Kevin should have been born, which was a grim coincidence. On her third visit I went with her, in a convoy of trucks delivering aid and clothes. That was a stunning experience. We were shocked at the first orphanage we visited because the woman in charge didn't really want our help at all. We had brought hundreds of parcels of food and clothes and medical supplies and she didn't seem at all interested. In fact, our arrival seemed to have irritated her. Then around 200 kids ran out to take a look at us. They all had closely-shaven heads because of the lice and, being naïve — I first thought that they were all boys. But there were girls among them too.

The conditions at that orphanage were bad, but the hospitals we went on to visit were much worse. One of the most striking things that hits you over there is that the hospitals are absolutely awful. They are in a disgraceful condition; the buildings smell and the rooms are dirty. They are just horrendous, and it seemed as though all the nurses, who appeared to be every bit as loving and caring as they are in Britain, had no teeth. They were all black and decayed. Dentistry costs money and there aren't many facilities anyway. What little money they have all goes on food.

We also had to deal with the corruption. When we were taking the food, clothes and medicine into the hospital, we were unloading it from the lorry and just as soon as we had stored it in a room, somebody was nicking things out of the back door. We lost 20 pairs of jeans in 10 minutes. They just disappeared. It was a land of bribes and back-handers.

There didn't seem to be any work over there but everybody appeared to be drinking and smoking all the time. They'd be drinking brandies in dingy cafés at 10.00 am. I don't know how they afforded it. The feeling when you fly out is one of immense relief, and normally you have to change planes in Zürich, which is antiseptically clean and affluent, a total culture shock.

We both saw Elly together. Our friend, Professor George Dragan, found out that there were three babies in a hospital in Honduras, so we travelled out there with some aid to see them. The three little mites were in a tiny room, swathed in blankets because there was no heating and they were all wearing horrible little bonnets. They were five weeks old and they had never been out of that awful room. The sewage system seemed to have given up, and the smell was appalling.

We had already decided that if we were to adopt a baby, then we would have a little girl, because we already had four boys and two girls. Two of the babies were girls — Elly and Rachel. That was just heart-breaking because we had to choose between the two and it meant leaving one behind. How can you choose between two beautiful little babies?

But it was as though God was taking a hand when we went back the next day. We were told by the matron that we could not have Rachel because she had already been adopted by a couple from Paris. So the choice was made for us and Elly became a member of our family. At that moment she started crying, so we picked her up and she became ours — she was a lovely little thing. It felt as though she had chosen us, not the other way round. She actually does look like one of the family. It took me all of two seconds to decide that I wanted to adopt a Romanian baby. It was one of those easy decisions that you never regret. I am a sucker for kids, I adore them. And when it came to it, how can you turn down a little baby like that?

But the process of adoption was far from easy. We first saw her when she was five weeks old but, by the time we went back for the initial adoption hearing, she was four-and-a-half months old. And she still had not been out of that room. The nurses just didn't have the time to take the children out. We took her outside into the fresh air for the first time in her young life and played with her in the grounds. She had never seen colours before and she seemed fascinated by the green grass. She had never even seen the sky and it was extraordinary to see her reactions. You just can't begin to imagine what her life would have been like if we hadn't been able to adopt her. It just doesn't bear thinking about. She would probably have gone to an institution and that would have been the end of her.

The legal formalities were very complicated. The Romanians were not easy to deal with, and often made things very difficult. I suppose it must have been difficult for them to have rich Westerners coming over to adopt their babies. There was also a strong backlash of public opinion against the Romanians for what they had done to this generation of children. There is no country in the world quite like it. Even poor African states who can't afford anything don't simply ignore a whole generation of children. But because of the pressure from world opinion, I think the Romanians did at least try to show the world that they were doing something about the problem.

The judge presiding over our hearing actually agreed to the adoption proceeding, but then put several obstacles in our way. We would arrive in Romania with all the statutory paperwork, and then find out that suddenly we had to have a letter from the Mayor of Derby saying that we were suitable parents. On another occasion, we arrived for the hearing with everything completed — our Romanian counsellor had prepared the submissions for us. We were then amazed when the judge said that there were some inaccuracies in the papers. He said that he was prepared to ignore them, however, and that we wouldn't have to go back to England to finalise the paperwork — as long as we brought him back a pair of jeans!

I thought the interpreter was joking, but he was absolutely serious. So when we arrived back the next time, we had to bring a pair of Levis with us. I went over three times, but Lesley made seven trips. It was an amazing experience for us to go through. I think we both found it very stressful and traumatic because it went on for so long, and we kept thinking that, at any point, our hopes could be dashed. And all the time we really thought of Elly as one of the family by then. I remember being on holiday in our caravan in Salcombe and trying to ring through to Romania to get hold of Professor George Dragan and ask him what on earth was going on, because there had been so many delays in the adoption process.

When I finally contacted him, he was just as exasperated as us. He simply told us, 'I can't do anything else.' I think he thought we were blaming him for the delays, but we weren't. We were just appalled and angered at the sheer frustration of the whole thing.

A wonderful nursing sister actually handed Elly over to us. We took photographs of her but she didn't want to smile because she had no teeth. We both carried Elly out of the orphanage and took her to the hotel. They made up a cot for her and she was so good, she didn't cry at all. We both met Elly's mother. She was a tiny little woman, we were amazed because Elly was quite solid even then. I think her mother was Hungarian/ Romanian.

One of the most moving aspects of the whole experience occurred during the adoption hearing in Romania. We had to stand up and swear that we would bring up Elly as our own daughter, in the same way as our own children. What upset me was that her natural mother had to be present, and she had to stand up and swear that she relinquished all claims and rights to Elly for ever, and that she understood she was never to see the child again. That made me cry. She was just terribly poor. The solicitor who saw our sadness said, 'Don't be upset because, in fact, her mother will be very pleased.' The mother had not seen the baby since her birth. She had signed her over for adoption because she was 17 and she already had one child. We agreed to send her a photograph of Elly every birthday.

When we finally went to fetch Elly, we flew out together to complete the last pieces of bureaucracy, but I had to leave to come back a day early because I was filming on *The Bill*.

I flew back on my own and Lesley brought Elly back with her. Even then, Lesley was hindered at the very last minute because the Romanian embassy wouldn't stamp her papers. She was due to catch a plane the following day. It seemed as though they were just being awkward for the sake of it. Thankfully, another official said 'Oh, do it,' and she was allowed to go.

I felt so elated when the ordeal was finally over and Elly was finally home. The joy in the house was amazing. The anticipation had been going on for so long and now Elly was finally here. The happiness from our kids was greater than you could possibly imagine. They were all delighted that their little sister had finally arrived.

When we had first talked about adopting, we had a family conference around the table and we talked about what we proposed to do. Lesley and I asked the children what they thought of the idea. Obviously, if one of the children had been against the plan then we would have had to take that into consideration, and I don't believe we would have gone ahead. But they were simply astounding. They were so enthusiastic about the idea that they made me feel very proud to have brought them up. They all agreed to the idea and immediately asked when we could start everything, and when Elly arrived she was just smothered with affection and love.

It must have been overwhelming for her because, until then, she only had a couple of other babies and four bare walls for company.

The fact that Elly looks a little like me as well is due to God. Initially, she didn't look like me at all. She has now grown into a wonderful, podgy little girl with dark eyes and a wicked smile — she's gorgeous.

CHAPTER TEN

THE BREAK-UP

Even now, I don't really understand exactly what went wrong with our marriage. I will hold my hands up and admit that it was mostly my fault that our marriage ended. If you want blame worked out on a percentage basis I would say that it is 80 per cent my fault, and I feel desperately guilty about it. But I can't even begin to understand why it happened, or why it finally had to end.

When I got married, I got married for life, I really did. Divorce was for other people, it certainly wasn't for me. I wanted to be with Lesley for the rest of my life. But it has gone tragically wrong and, above all, I am desperately sorry for that.

I can talk about it now but at the time it was

absolutely shattering. I was numb for months and months. Unless your marriage has completely broken down you never believe it is going to finish like that. Unless you really hate each other, I think you believe it will be all right in the end. I know I did.

In some ways I still can't accept that it's over. I find myself thinking that it's all a horrible nightmare and I'll wake up back at home with Lesley and the kids. I still dream that Lesley will ring up and say, 'I want you back,' and the bad dream will be over. Now I know that's only a dream. I have to accept it.

It takes two to form a relationship but only one to finish it. My overwhelming feeling is just that I am desperately sorry that it has ended. But I think maybe I was attempting the impossible. I was living in Derby and working in London and trying to get home every night to be with the family; I finished up just about tearing myself in half. I managed it for a long while, but I couldn't do it for ever. Now I just wish I had never tried.

We were very happy until a couple of years ago. I would say that we had one of the happiest marriages possible. I had always wanted a really big, happy family and I was delighted with the one I had. If you could buy children off the shelf I would have had more and so would Lesley. The love of children was something Lesley and I shared and never ever argued about. That is why, even after we already had six wonderful children, we adopted Elly.

But sometimes your life goes in directions you don't realise. It didn't happen overnight by any means but, a couple of years ago, the pressures of work and travel and family began to take its toll on me.

Gradually, I just became more and more worn down

by it all. My health wasn't great and, stupidly, I used drink as a prop, something to pick me up and give me a lift. I would reach for a drink to give me a little boost when I was down.

Lesley had opened a delicatessen near our home in Duffield. She is a tremendous worker and all the time we have been together she has coupled running the family home with running a business, from all sorts of catering enterprises to a stationer's shop. She had worked at the delicatessen for some time and, although it was not doing particularly well, she could see that the business had great potential.

She has always had a flair for catering. Even when we first met, she was running a business called Thyme and Thyme Again, which offered the sort of classy private catering she is very good at. She started the shops when we moved to Derbyshire.

I bought her the delicatessen for £25,000 just over two years ago. I was happy enough to pay that. The money came from the pantomime I did at Birmingham Hippodrome. I absolutely knackered myself doing it, but I saved £39,000.

I managed to get Su Pollard and Ray Meagher, who plays Alf in *Home and Away*, to help open the deli, and we were both full of optimism. I didn't think that we were going to make a fortune, I was just trying to help Lesley.

I knew how much she wanted the shop and I bought it because I knew having her own business meant so much to Lesley. It was just my way of saying I love you. I realised that, although she wanted it, she would never ask me for it. She was already preparing delicacies for the owner of the deli at the time, but the business was doing badly and it soon came up for sale.

She could see that there was a real opportunity to build an excellent business with proper effort and investment. She asked the owner if she could buy it and he agreed. We were both delighted with the deal. It's a lovely shop, a proper deli that is a real asset to the village.

But right from the outset, the shop caused all sorts of problems for Lesley because we steadily lost money. Lesley had to put all her time and energy into it and look after the kids at the same time, so we hadn't much time to talk.

She worked her socks off and so did I. Two people who are totally exhausted cannot make a great partnership and the happy times just seemed to fade away without either of us noticing. In spite of Lesley's efforts, the shop struggled and I had to put some more money into it.

While doing the pantomime in Birmingham, I contracted bronchitis to go with my diabetes. My health deteriorated fast, all adding to the stress. I felt rough, but I love doing panto so I didn't mind.

Now, in the cold light of separation, I think it was a bit mean of her to let me buy the shop if she truly thought that things were so bad between us. Lesley has told me since that she wanted to have a business behind her if we were to split up. She reckoned it was a sort of insurance if I ever cleared off.

That seems a bit cold and cynical to me because, at the time, nothing was further from my mind. I thought we were happily married; too busy to have enough time for each other, certainly, but still happily married. And I think the truth is that things were never anything like as bad as Lesley has painted them since.

I have always been a little soft and stupid where money is concerned, but it never entered my brain that she wasn't 100 per cent committed to the marriage. I say again, I thought we were happy. If I had thought we weren't, I don't know whether I would have bought Lesley the shop.

I think it was quite a generous thing to do. I invested money in her businesses because I loved her — I didn't want anything out of it, I just did it because I thought it made her happy.

There are ups and downs in any marriage but, in spite of a few rows, I thought that we were happy. Lesley says now that there were times, earlier in our marriage, when she was unhappy. She says she was pleased to leave London. She said she desperately wanted to be out in the country.

I bought Lesley the shop in the November, and it was only in the following July that I received the letter from the solicitors demanding that I move out of the house.

The pressure really built up when I took on another panto at the Birmingham Hippodrome, *Jack and the Beanstalk*, doing two shows a day. I would perform solidly for six days, and then on the seventh I would rush down to London to film *The Bill*. I did that for six weeks.

That was when everything came to a head. I simply had not realised just how serious my diabetes had become, and just when I needed to be strong, my health crumbled. That played a major part in my downfall. I just felt as though I could not keep going without some assistance, and used the booze more and more as a crutch to help me through a difficult time. I was totally knackered and thought I could use a drink or two to give me a little boost.

I took the panto because I love it but, to be honest, I was knackered even before that. It wasn't the money. I love doing panto and one of my big failings is finding it very hard to say 'No' when people ask me to do things. At the moment, the powers that be at *The Bill* dictate that the cast are not allowed to do them, but as soon as the ban is lifted I'll be reaching for my tights.

Paul Elliott, the 'King of Pantos', reckons that I'm the second-best villain in the country, behind the other television policeman John Nettles, which I suppose is some sort of accolade. But it was doing six weeks without a single day off that destroyed me. I was doing ridiculous things, such as jumping on the last train to London after the final performance to be in the studios at 7.00 am for *The Bill*'s filming. It was non-stop work and Lesley and I never saw each other. It was crazy. But, at the time, you think you can handle it. And it was the money from the panto that bought Lesley her business in the first place.

Lesley and I just became ships that pass in the night. We were both working very hard. I would be getting in from the pantomime at 2.00 am, having finished work at about 11.00 pm and having had a meal. Lesley would get up at 5.00 am or 6.00 am to start in the shop at 8.00 am. We just stopped communicating — it's very difficult to talk if you never see each other.

Yet even at this time, just weeks before she ordered me to move out of the house, I felt that Lesley and I were still very close. It was one of the proudest nights of my life when Princess Anne came to a Royal Charity Performance of the pantomime and I had my whole family, including my mum and Lesley's mum and dad, there in the audience.

It was a tremendous night. You could not have found

a prouder man in the country. Lesley and the kids had already seen the panto but they came again. I was introduced to Princess Anne afterwards. The whole occasion was glittering. We are all great Royalists and I was so delighted that the evening happened. When I was younger, I never thought I would do anything like that.

Afterwards, we all went out for a meal together and, if ever a family was happy together, it was us that night. That's what makes what happened afterwards so hard for me to comprehend. We were all so proud of each other and I knew I couldn't have kept going and achieved so much without those people.

That is what upsets me so much about my mother-in-law because she wasn't always hard work — she could be lovely, absolutely charming and a delight to be with. And she was lovely that day when she said how proud she was of me. It made me feel about 20-feet tall.

The trouble was that we both slipped back into the old routine afterwards. After that magical night, I was soon so tired again that I would get home in a state of complete exhaustion. I had no relaxation of any kind. I don't play golf so I can't go out with the boys and relax on the course or anything like that.

Even after the panto had finished and I resumed *The Bill* full-time, I would get off the train at 9.30 pm and then I'd nip into the Midland Hotel to have a couple of beers while I was waiting for a taxi. I wouldn't get home until 11.00 pm, and then I'd be gone again at the crack of dawn.

So Lesley would see me at my very worst point in the day, when I was grumpy and knackered, and when I had literally got nothing left.

Initially, I was only contracted to *The Bill* for six

months, but gradually a six-month job became several years. I made a decision very early on that I would go home at night whenever I possibly could to kiss the children goodnight. I did not want to stay in London and miss seeing my family.

A lot of blokes would have just got a flat and gone out on the town in London and had a jolly good time, but I am not like that. I have always been a very family-orientated man and, although I know it sounds crazy now I am apart from them, in my heart, I still am. I have always taken such pride and joy in my family. That is the real me.

I admit that the big problem about our marriage was me. I accept the vast majority of the blame for our split. It makes me very sad and very ashamed. I tried to do too much and I failed. I used booze to keep me going. I probably never came home as soon as I should have done.

My only defence is that mine is quite a stressful job. Tosh might look crumpled and relaxed on TV, but it takes an awful lot of tension and effort to get him to appear so easy-going. I love acting but I have to work hard for a performance. I know it looks effortless and it should. But by the time I was travelling home, I would be completely exhausted and in desperate need of some way to unwind.

The rows seemed to became longer and more frequent at that time, and I found myself resenting the aggravation. It just seemed totally unfair; I was working my socks off for the family and for Lesley, and then she expected me to be bright and romantic when I got home.

With the benefit of hindsight, I realise that I should have had three or four nights in a hotel and then come home fresh and full of beans at the weekend.

I regret it now, but then I wouldn't have been happy staying away. I would have missed the family far too much. I'd even come home on the 2.00am train and go back on the 5.00am, just so that I could kiss the kids goodnight even though they were fast asleep. That's what I wanted, that's what I needed. I'm not pretending I did it just for them; I did it for myself, as well.

Lesley was unhappy and she told me so. But, to be honest, I didn't really listen. There didn't seem to be anything I could do about working hard. Actors in long-running shows are on a kind of treadmill. You have to keep on going, everyone gets tired and stressed from time to time. You just have to get your head down and do the work.

Actors are much too insecure to ask for less work. In any case, you're either in *The Bill* or you're not. You can't leave early because you want to get home to see your family.

But I know I did other stupid things. Sometimes, I would go out on a Saturday night for a Chinese takeaway and pop into the pub on the way, and then come back an hour-and-a-half later with a very cold Chinese.

That was wrong and thoughtless and I would quite rightly be told off for that. The kids would end up eating something else with Lesley and I'd be left with the cold Chinese.

I can see now that that is unacceptable behaviour. But, even in my darkest moments, I never really believed that it was upsetting Lesley that much. I never imagined that it could have led to this.

My epitaph will be 'He tried to do too much'. I was

permanently travelling, becoming more and more knackered, and then drinking too much to try to keep going — I needed to be with my family, and to sleep in my own bed.

The trouble was that, as the rows built up, I was regularly doing that alone as Lesley moved into the spare room. I was shocked by that. There was no huge drama. She just announced one night that she was going to sleep in the other room. I thought it was just another temporary blip.

I might sound naïve, but it honestly never entered my mind that things would go downhill from there. I just thought it was a bit of a bad patch and that things would soon get back to normality.

My life just seemed to get incredibly full. Even if you've had a hard week at work, when someone asks you to play cricket on Sunday for the Lords' Taverners to raise money for handicapped children, it's very hard to say 'No'. I always said 'Yes'.

I do a lot of charity work, usually one event a week, and I believe it is very important. But I know Lesley and the kids were getting fed up with it after I had already done a full week's filming.

I was exhausted. I used to spend Sunday morning writing my column for the local paper, which I can't do very quickly, and by Sunday afternoon I was still absolutely exhausted. It seems so clear now that I just wasn't spending enough time with the family. But I wasn't working like that for fun — *The Bill* was paying the mortgage.

I just thought I could cope physically. It was the diabetes that really took the wind out of my sails because that drains you of energy. I first found out about that when I was 40, but it tends to hit you hardest when you're at your most vulnerable.

The Bill is a great job; good work and plenty of it. But for me, it was in the wrong place. At one point, Lesley even offered to move down to London to be nearer my work. We talked about that, but I refused because the kids were doing well at school, and coming up to their GCSE and 'A'-level exams.

I thought that if we stayed as we were, with me doing all the travelling, then the only person who suffered would be me and Lesley was prepared to let me do that. I understood perfectly. The family was settled. It's a lovely house and she wanted to stay there.

When we first moved to Derby I was working all over the country, in cities like Birmingham, Manchester, Leeds and London. But as soon as we settled in Derbyshire, it was sod's law that all my work was suddenly London-based — I had a year's run in a play in the West End and then *The Bill*. Over the period I steadily became more tired and run down. I moved into my 40s and couldn't physically do some of the things I had done easily as a younger man.

And my diabetes became worse. That can be really debilitating. It is now controlled, fortunately, but at the time I was doing far too much. My schedule was very heavy on *The Bill* and I also did the pantomimes for the last three years. They are incredibly demanding. I was drinking more. Being tired and overworked I was also grumpy. I'm only human.

But that was only in the last year or so. Until then, I was always a happy and very occasional drunk. Drink made me happier and more gregarious and I never used to depend on it.

I freely admit that I have had times when I have been

drunk. Sometimes, I have not been able to remember the night before very clearly, but those occasions are very rare. I have never lost complete days like some people. I have never gone to bed and not known what I've done the night before.

And Lesley has accused me of being a violent drunk, which I deny. It is one of the most hurtful things she has said. I have hardly ever smacked my children. You can count on the fingers of one hand the number of times I have had to use a smack. And I have never, ever hit Lesley. We have had rows, blazing rows, but I have never hit her. I have never wanted to.

Very often, our disagreements were nothing to do with drinking. Very often, we would both be completely sober. We had a few angry rows over the years like anyone else. For a long time, the cause of any trouble between us was our parents and the ways in which we felt manipulated by them, and their apparent desire to interfere in our lives. They caused an awful lot of problems between us, particularly when the children were involved.

A couple need to be left alone to sort things out themselves, but it seemed as though we were never given this space. I always felt it was easy for Lesley's parents to get at me because Mark and Sophie weren't my natural children. They knew that if they wanted to upset me, they could do it by favouring one of those two. It would annoy me every time.

For a long time, we used to say that the only thing we argued about was the in-laws — not my coming home late or drinking, but it was invariably my mother and Lesley's parents coming between us. My mum was on her own, and my in-laws' marriage didn't seem to be the greatest, so all three of them seemed to have plenty of time and energy to focus on us and the grandchildren.

Lesley's sister is very wise. She and her partner see her parents sparingly. But I am a gregarious bloke and I always loved the idea of a great big, happy family with everyone getting on well together. It just never seemed quite possible.

Things were going from bad to worse. We weren't talking too much and Lesley had already relegated herself to the other bedroom. Then, one day, she was walking out of the front door and, as she was leaving, said, 'I'll see you when you get back.' But there was something strange about the way she said it. When I got to work at *The Bill* studios that day, one of the security men said, 'Your wife rang to make sure you have got the letter.' And there it was, sitting in my pigeon hole. It was from a firm of solicitors in Nottingham, spelling out in cold lawyers' language that Lesley wanted me to move out. It was an awful shock to me.

The letter said I must leave 'the matrimonial home' and get treatment for what they called my 'problem with alcohol' or she would issue divorce proceedings. Lesley was going to be away for the weekend for me to 'return in order to collect any personal belongings'. I had tears in my eyes as I read it. Even though things had not been going well between us, I could not believe that it had come to this.

The letter threatened that if I did not move out instantly, I would face the publicity of a divorce. 'Mrs Lloyd has particularly asked us to draw your attention to the fact that if proceedings are issued, then they must be heard in Open Court. This means that the hearing will be open to the public and consequently also to the Press. Mrs Lloyd is very aware of the effect that such adverse publicity could have on your career. She has no wish at all to expose you to this. If you do not leave voluntarily then the proceedings will be issued and Mrs Lloyd will be unable to protect you from the consequences of your own behaviour.'

That letter was a huge shock to me. I wandered around in a bit of a trance for the rest of that day, and that night I lay awake, stunned. I couldn't understand it. Never, ever during our angriest rows had I imagined Lesley would stop talking to me and start talking to solicitors. I didn't ever think she would go that far. I just think she had been listening to the wrong people.

That letter really knocked me sideways. I went as white as a sheet and rang Lesley and asked, 'What on earth have you done this for?'

'I've had enough,' she replied.

It was a Thursday, and my orders were to collect my stuff that weekend, and don't come back.

I had to fulfil a list of conditions: I had to move out; there would be no publicity. What a joke that was. Thanks to Lesley and the popularity of *The Bill*, our problems have never been out of the papers. I would have to stop drinking, and I would have to receive treatment for my drinking, and so on. I fulfilled them all. I went though the list and did everything. I was desperate to save my marriage.

My mum took me in. It was terrible, really, for both of us. Mums are mums. My mum is 78 and she is the best mum in the world, but the last thing she wanted was her sick and emotionally devastated son bringing all his problems back home. It was very hard for her to accept.

My diabetes was getting worse and I had developed

a foot infection when I was doing the panto. I was given antibiotics for it, but unknown to me, my diabetes was getting worse. I was so busy and upset I wasn't taking proper care of myself.

It ended up with me being rushed into the Nuffield hospital, where I had another shock. I was given only a 20 per cent chance of saving my right foot. It was that bad. About four days later, I learned that it was healing.

When I got back to my mum's, I was a complete mess. I couldn't walk because of my foot. I stopped drinking there and then because I was determined to abide by the conditions set out in the letter. It was a dreadful time. My mum is great, but it wasn't easy living with her. She has lived on her own for a long time and very quickly we started to get on each other's nerves. I used to pray for her to go out shopping. She looked after me, but it wasn't easy for either of us.

I was so shocked at what had happened. One minute I had a lovely home and a big happy family, and the next minute I'm living with my old mum. I just couldn't take it in at first. For years, the Lloyd family had been written up in the papers as television's happiest family and, as far as I was concerned, all the stories were absolutely true. I am not ashamed to say that I cried myself to sleep most nights. I just couldn't believe that my life had somehow been completely taken away from me. And it would have been bad enough if we could have kept the pain to ourselves. But we couldn't.

Bad news always travels fast and the papers soon picked up the story. Lesley's idea of 'no publicity' seemed to be to tell the tabloids everything they wanted to know. I was absolutely reeling. I've never been in such a state. From being a father positioned at the centre of his family, I had suddenly become an outsider. I had heard of divorced fathers complaining about the agonies of strictly limited visiting hours, but I had no idea just how ghastly it would be.

Lesley and I came to an agreement, whereby I would take the children out once a week, either to the pictures, to the theatre or for a meal. And I used to take one of them to the football as well. I know that sort of arrangement works for some people, but right from the start I just couldn't bear it. Seeing the children for a brief time and then being parted from them again was purgatory. On one occasion, I remember Lesley pulling into the big McDonald's at Markeaton Island in Derby to drop the children off with me.

I was so upset I just burst into tears. Lesley looked at me. She just drove off without looking back.

It was hard for all of us. Thank goodness the young ones didn't understand everything, but they had seen and heard a lot of rows between mummy and daddy. They knew that mummy and daddy weren't happy and that daddy was living with their grandmother. It must have been upsetting and baffling for them. But that day they seemed fine. They were playing on the chutes in the playground, and I just sat there with tears running down my face, crying like a baby. I just couldn't help it.

I suppose the incident that sparked even more trouble happened when Lesley was away in America visiting our eldest son, Mark. My in-laws were at the house again looking after the children. On the Saturday, I was going to take one of the children to watch Derby County play — a very important fixture in my personal diary — and it was little Edward's turn.

He was just seven and he was looking forward to coming. I was out in the morning when I received this rather formal message from my mother-in-law saying, 'You'll have to pick him up by one o'clock because we are going out.'

I made sure I got there in plenty of time. I arrived at 12.45pm to pick him up and, when I got to the house, they had gone out and taken Edward with them. I couldn't believe it. The house was locked and empty. That made me furious. I went back to get my lift. I was livid all the way through the football match because I love all my kids and I wanted Edward to be with me at the game.

When I got back, I had a dreadful row with my in-laws. I couldn't believe they could do that to me and I said so. I shouted, 'This is my son, you have no right to stop him coming with me.' We had an awful scene. They knew things were not good between Lesley and me. In frustration, I hit the bathroom door. I stormed out. Unfortunately, the kids saw all this. Upsetting the children is the last thing I ever wanted to do, but I was just so angry I flipped. I just thought that the actions of my in-laws had been disgraceful. Naturally, our relationship wasn't helped when Lesley had the story reported to her, gory details and all.

For six months I tried everything, and I mean everything, to put my marriage back together. There was no court order forcing me to move out, but I did, to give us both a bit of space. I spent six months living away from home, desperately trying to win Lesley back. For most of that time, although I did not dare admit it even to myself, I was somehow confident that we would get back together. I kept remembering how happy we had been together. It wasn't just an 'OK' marriage where we had gradually became bored with each other, it was a fantastic marriage that seemed to grow better and better as more and more children arrived.

I didn't just love Lesley, I worshipped her, and she always seemed to feel the same way. I never looked at another woman, not because I'm any kind of saint, but because I didn't want to. Paul Newman said something once about never wanting to nibble a cheap cut of meat while he had steak at home, and that is exactly how I felt.

Even when I moved out I never stopped loving Lesley. Sure, I didn't understand her, but I was still crazy about her. For a while, things were quite amicable on that level. Sometimes, I even went back into the house after I delivered the children back and occasionally she asked me to stay for a meal. I kept telling myself things were not completely lost. When I went to Bosnia to take some toys to refugee children towards the end of the year, I rang Lesley up to say where I was and gave her contact numbers in case of any family emergency, and it began to feel as though I was just away from home like old times.

I tried desperately to put things right with Lesley, but it just never happened. We often talked but I could never reach her. I think she had been advised by someone that the best way to behave was to have nothing to do with me, to cut me off completely in order to make me come to what she thought was my senses.

At first, I used to ask if I could meet the kids from school when I was off work. Initially, she agreed and then later she would suddenly say that I couldn't do it any more. She said, 'I know what you're trying to do.

You're trying to wheedle your way back in.' In a way, I was, but what was I expected to do? I was desperately trying to fight for my marriage. I would have done anything. Even my mum, who is in many ways my biggest critic, said that she felt I had done everything I could to put things right after the bust-up. Every now and then I felt Lesley begin to warm towards me, and I would start to think that there was a chance we might patch things up. Then I would ask her out for a meal or to come to the cinema, but the answer would always be 'No'. She was always distant and a barrier appeared between us.

It was so strange for me because our house was always so happy. A big, happy family house. I can't understand the way Lesley behaved. I pleaded with her to come with me to Relate and talk to marriage guidance counsellors, but she never would. She wouldn't even consider it. During that awful six-month period when I was living with my mother, trying to fulfil all of Lesley's conditions and desperately hoping I could rebuild my marriage, it seemed to me that Lesley was under the influence of others who weren't prepared to let me back into my own family.

Even before then, every time I came home it seemed that Lesley's mother was always there. Then Lesley would say that her parents would be coming for someone's birthday or another occasion, of which there are plenty in our family. In the end, it meant that I could never really enjoy a proper conversation with Lesley without it constantly being passed back to her mother. It seemed as though we would meet and begin to build things up a little, and then my mother-in-law would meddle. It just didn't help.

The Press made an already dreadful time an awful lot

worse. They would be hanging round outside my mother's house, and they were so rude and objectionable that they nearly gave a 78-year-old lady a heart-attack. And they were round camped outside my house causing trouble as well. One day, I took Poppy with me to watch Derby and we were walking down our street when she turned to me and said, 'There's a man down there taking photographs, Daddy.' A photographer was waiting in a car outside the King's Head, taking shots of us from across the road. The story was splashed across the papers saying, 'Here's Tosh with his new girlfriend,' until they found out that Poppy was my daughter, and then it was 'Tosh is back at home everything is back to normal.' After that, Lesley went potty and accused me of setting up the photograph to get back into our house somehow. It was absolute rubbish.

Throughout that six months, I did not touch anything alcoholic. I was determined to get her back. It was only when I went to Bosnia for the *News of the World* just before Christmas 1995 that I had my first drink for six months. It was literally only a glass or two; it was too important to risk.

It was while I was in hospital that the divorce papers arrived. They weren't exactly a great 'get well' card. I honestly believe that Lesley did it as a form of shock therapy, to try to shock me out of my current state into a complete change of lifestyle. I was basically working far too hard and I was knackered. I needed a rest and I was ill with the diabetes.

I was lying in bed with my foot up. My diabetic consultant, Ian Peacock, and another consultant were with me when the matron announced that a visitor had come to see me. A private detective came in with the divorce papers. He gave them to me and said cheerily, 'I hope you get better soon.' Looking back, I suppose it was quite a comical situation but I still can't quite appreciate the funny side.

Then Christmas came and it was brought home to me just where I figured in Lesley's future plans for the Lloyd family. Lesley went to her sister's house at Alderley Edge for Christmas Day and I was invited to join them. Perhaps 'invite' is too strong a word. It was more a case of being permitted to be there, and I was given strict times and conditions to which I was forced to adhere, like a prisoner out on parole.

I was told to arrive at 10.00 am and leave at 6.00 pm and to behave myself. I should have known that this was scarcely the recipe for a happy, relaxed Christmas, but I decided to go, even though it meant swallowing a lot of pride. I was desperate to spend the day with the children even if it meant confronting the rest of the family. I booked myself into a cheerless hotel nearby where I was the only guest. My brother-in-law came to fetch me and he gave me a shock by telling me how sorry he was that my divorce was going through. I knew Lesley had filed the initial papers, but this casual remark was the first indication I had had that the divorce was actually proceeding. So I was feeling pretty shattered even before I arrived.

When we reached the house, I said to him, 'Just do me one favour. Please don't sit me anywhere near my mother-in-law at the dining table.' When I got inside, I saw that my worst fears had come true — with the best will in the world, I just couldn't face it. It was bad enough to be allowed there on sufferance only at certain times, but I simply refused to sit next to her. It wasn't exactly a great start to the celebrations, and the mood was difficult from then on. Lesley said afterwards that had I behaved differently, I would have been invited for Boxing Day. As it turned out, I wasn't, so I spent the day on my own in my room because I happened to be the only guest in the hotel at the time.

I realised that everyone else was spending Christmas with their families. There were no trains or buses running back to Derby, so I couldn't even get back to my mother. It was horrendous, one of the lowest points of my life. I felt very sorry for myself and I went for a long walk on my own; my depression grew and grew. My family was only a short distance away and I could not be with them. I think I cried myself to sleep like a baby that night.

I am not sure if Lesley wanted to punish me for coming home so late and drunk so often, but I believe she has got a great anger in her, which has built up over the years. I think she felt that she had been betrayed by me. And, in a way, she had, and it is my biggest regret that I have hurt her and the kids because they have been my life and, in my heart I feel they still are my life. I think about them every day.

I was then told that I was divorced. I received the decree nisi and having trained as a solicitor, I knew that six weeks after that, on St Valentine's Day, ironically, the divorce would be absolute. That was it. Our marriage was over. I pleaded with Lesley but she was adamant. There was not a thing that I could say or do that would change her mind.

For several weeks at the start of 1996, I had almost nothing at all to do with Lesley. I was very, very upset all over again. Even though the visiting arrangements were dreadful, at least there was still some contact between us, but she said she wanted nothing more to do with me. I now believed that it was finally over. I suppose I was in shock. I didn't know how you were supposed to behave, but I didn't want any more screaming matches or vicious headlines. I wanted to cling on to seeing the children and I somehow started to accept, for the first time, that I had lost Lesley for good.

CHAPTER ELEVEN

RITA

I then met Rita Hudson. I think I was at my lowest ebb in March 1996. The happy family man was in danger of becoming a very bitter bachelor and, to avoid that, I was trying to throw myself into my work. Being Tosh Lines suddenly became a great deal more appealing than being Kevin Lloyd. And many of my friends on the programme were extremely caring and supportive.

And I still went to watch Derby. The club has been part of my life since I was a youngster and when everything is going wrong, you're inclined to stick with old friends.

At first, I thought Rita was the wife of one of the football club's directors. She was in a group of supporters I knew and we met properly towards the end of the month. We just talked football at first, and slowly we got to know each other. I wasn't trying to hide anything — there was nothing to hide. Then a newspaper printed a picture of us sitting side by side in the crowd. It was a good story but it wasn't true — the picture was cleverly edited by removing a friend of mine, John Cheadle, who was sitting between us.

At the time, we hadn't done more than smile at each other and exchange the odd word about Marco Gabbiadini's grim goal drought. But, slowly, we became friends. I learned that she wasn't married and that she came to the matches because her daughter was married to Derby's boss and saviour, Lionel Pickering, who was a good friend of mine. The last thing I was looking for at the time was another relationship.

The only person I had really talked to was Hilary Jennings, the girl I fell in love with and jilted nearly 30 years before when I went off to drama school. Hilary was still very, very special to me. She is now happily married with three children, and lives just outside Huddersfield. But our relationship was just about the most important thing in my life before I met Lesley. We were so young but I have never forgotten her.

When I broke up with Lesley, Hilary was the first person I rang. I hadn't spoken to her for 26 years, but when I was really despairing after I had moved out, she was the person I called. She was lovely. There were no angry recriminations about me letting her down all those years before. She just listened to me. She's a psychiatric nurse now, so she is probably ideally qualified to talk to me.

It was the most extraordinary conversation you

could ever have. Of course, she did tell me how devastated she was when we split up. We wondered what would have happened if I'd remained in Derby and we had stayed together.

To be honest, I think I would be dead by now if I'd stayed working as a solicitor's clerk, at least from the neck upwards. I'd be 48, even fatter, and bored senseless by going to the same courts and doing the same type of cases all the time.

But that conversation with Hilary was great. We talked and talked and talked, about what it was like when we parted, about our lives and our families since then, and about my problems. I broke her heart, and I have always felt very guilty about that. It was extraordinary to talk about that after 26 years. It was as if the time had never passed. She was just as fresh and funny and kind as I remembered.

She is a beautiful person, very caring, and that is why she has became a psychiatric nurse and is now a sister — she always had a vocation for caring for people. She is very happily married now, so I did not want to cause any upset or misunderstandings by actually meeting her. We had three very long phonecalls and they were really helpful to me in my depressed and miserable state. I didn't want to push it, but it was great to ring Hilary, someone I had loved and someone I really felt I could still trust completely, even after all those years.

It was marvellous. I would have understood if she had just slammed the phone down after the way I had treated her, but thank goodness she didn't. The conversation was very therapeutic. At last I was able to say I was sorry for treating her so badly. I've harboured a lot of guilt about what happened and I have never forgotten her. Funnily enough, everyone who has met Lesley and Hilary says how much they look alike. Talking to her again was a real trip down Memory Lane. She said the sweetest things to me and I drew enormous strength from her. A few weeks later, I had to stay in an hotel not far from where she lived and I even thought about knocking on her door. But I decided against it. Our memories are best left as they are.

Rita was not a memory though. She just seemed a bright and funny woman who loved to talk about football. After we had hit the headlines together, I tried to apologise but she didn't seem to mind. And there seemed no point in trying to hide anything. Millions of newspaper readers already assumed we were locked in a torrid affair.

I was very low and lonely after months on my own and I asked her out for a meal. I didn't really plan to ask her out, it just happened. I would never have asked another woman out if I had not been certain that my marriage was over. Lesley had told me herself that it was finished and that we were divorced. So I asked Rita out. But I was on tenterhooks waiting for her answer. Thankfully, she said 'Yes', but I don't think either of us knew what to expect.

Going out on that first date was like being a teenager again. If you haven't courted or even asked a girl out in 22 years, then you're likely to feel pretty awkward and I certainly did! That is what I had been dreading. When I realised my marriage was over I thought, 'Have I got a life ahead of me? Am I going to spend the rest of my life on my own?'

It takes a lot to get to know somebody. Particularly when you get older. That feeling about the difficulty of getting to know somebody new again can be very daunting and, afterwards, Rita told me that was exactly how she felt as well. It's very hard to have the confidence to be able to trust somebody again. Rita's marriage lasted for 12 years and mine for 22. They both lasted an awfully long time, a huge chunk of your life being with the same person.

I was very, very nervous. I went to her flat in Ashbourne and picked her up, and from there we went to a wine bar for a meal. Fortunately, when we sat down together I was not that tongue-tied because I had had a few beers beforehand to relax me. She said afterwards that she felt exactly the same. All we had talked about before was football at a match, so a proper meeting could have been a complete disaster. I feared the biggest mutual embarrassment ever, which could have happened.

I was terrified we would sit there blank-faced and unable to talk to each other. That was my personal nightmare. She could have been really boring. I could have been really boring. But it turned out that we clicked straight away. We made each other laugh. All evening. And I think it was the first time we had laughed for a long time. We weren't lovers or anything like it.

But we were friends and we gave each other confidence and a much-needed boost. I certainly wanted to see her again and she seemed to agree to a second date.

A little time after that, my solicitor rang up and said, 'You'd better sit down, I've got a bit of a shock for you. You are not divorced.' Lesley hadn't made it absolute. I was told that the decree absolute was on 14 February, and I first went out with Rita at the end of

March. I was still married. Lesley had shocked me again. I was beginning to expect surprises.

Everything changed when Rita came on the scene. The chilly calm that had characterised the mood between Lesley and I was shattered. To say she was upset was an understatement. First, Lesley sent me a bitter letter in which she enclosed her wedding rings, which had all been cut up. That really devastated me. That was one of the most hurtful things that I have ever experienced. Even after everything else it was a real body blow.

In the letter she wrote, 'You will never know how much I loved you. But Rita has seen an end to that. Here are your rings back. You will never know how much they meant to me.' It was a letter that really got to me. I know I will never really get over that, I just have to try to bury it deep down inside somewhere.

But I couldn't bury her more public outburst of anger — a devastating series of articles in the *Daily Mirror* which blasted me as a violent, bullying drunk. I thought I was ready for anything, but those hideous headlines really dazed me.

Day after day, I saw my happy marriage twisted and distorted into headlines that painted me as a loathsome monster who appeared to have been completely paralytic for 20 years.

I was shattered when I saw the stories. Lesley is supposed to have received £35,000 for those horrendous stories and I hope she thought it was worth it. Part of me died when I read it. I thought of my children sitting in class with other youngsters, having to cope with seeing their parents' problems splashed across double-page spreads. But I was also completely baffled.

She didn't need the money. Her family is well-off and I have provided well for her.

I was offered a lot of money by the *News of the World*, to name but one, to give my version and respond to Lesley's claims. I refused. I never said a single word to anyone despite the offers. I could certainly have done with the money, but I would never stoop to that level. Obviously, I have some very strong feelings about Lesley after everything that has happened, but I am not going to start laying into her in print. I am only writing this book because I want to keep control of every word and to tell the true story of my love for Lesley. I want my children to know that their daddy still cares for them and loves them, even if he doesn't see them.

Until Lesley spoke to the papers, I thought I really knew her as well as any man can know a woman. We have laughed and cried together for more than 20 years; we have brought up seven terrific children; we have wept together as we buried our daughter; we have stood side by side in a grim Romanian orphanage and fought together to bring little Elly back to our home. And I never dreamt she was capable of doing anything like that to me.

It wasn't really the rows, the drinking or the coming home late that really triggered Lesley's public rage. It was when another woman appeared on the scene, that is when she sold her story to the paper. They had been pestering her to write her story and have a go at me for ages and, after they had run a story about me and Rita, eventually she gave in.

It looked awful in print and it made me feel wretched. I don't know how Lesley felt, I haven't asked her. An enormous number of people have offered me their sympathy, and asked how could she have done that. But in spite of how much it hurt, I would not try to hit back. She did it for her own private reasons, and she has to live with that.

Were Lesley's stories about us completely true? That is surely what many people must be asking. The short and honest answer is 'No'. They were nothing like the truth.

What she said about our arguments was partly true and it was true that I had once slapped Sophie across the face. The circumstances were conveniently left out, though. Everything else was distorted and twisted. And the stuff about me being violent was simply untrue.

Lesley said in the articles that I ripped clothes from her and pinched her arms as though it happened on a daily basis. That must be one of the wildest exaggerations. We were once holding each other during a row and, as she pushed away, her jumper did rip. Once. Even during our most heated confrontations, I never hit Lesley or even remotely considered it.

Over the preceding months, I had pleaded endlessly for the chance of a reconciliation. Lesley always said 'No'. I had even sent a solicitor's letter saying that I wanted a reconciliation. When she told me we were divorced and that it was finally over, I pleaded again. I begged her to try again, for the sake of the children if not for me.

But she just did not listen. And then, when she heard that I had someone else in my life, she lashed out to hurt me. I couldn't believe it. I was hurt of course but I was more worried about the effect on the children. I chose to become an actor and I was delighted when I became widely known, but that is me and my life. My young children did not choose to live their lives in public.

It is very difficult for Rita to come into my life with all that sadness just behind me. But I am an actor and at least I have been able to put on a brave face in public and look as though I am perky and optimistic. But deep down I have been deeply hurt and still am. It is not all due to Lesley, but also because of the circumstances and the inevitable repercussions. Rita has helped me enormously to get through what has been the most difficult period of my life. Caring is the best single word to describe her, I think. She is an extremely caring, lovable lady, and she has an enormous warmth and understanding that helps her to care for other people. She is very selfless.

She works as a counsellor and has had a lot of tragedy in her life. She has been through a divorce herself and has had to work through a great deal of sadness and upset, which seems to have made her very understanding. But our initial liking for each other was not based on a mutual moaning between us, but a mutual attraction. We enjoyed each other's company. It wasn't really like having a shoulder to cry on, we just had a good time together. She is a year younger than me. When I met her she had been separated for just over a year and is now divorced, she has a daughter, Melanie, who is 30.

The whole experience has knocked me for six, particularly Lesley's enthusiasm for washing every single item of dirty linen in the tabloid newspapers. At one very low point, a landlord in Ashbourne was sympathising with me one night. He said his marriage had gone wrong and he felt he couldn't go anywhere in Ashbourne because everybody knew about it. Then he looked at me and said, 'What must it be like for you?'

It was awful because everybody was aware of my situation, but I was very pleasantly surprised by the incredible amount of sympathy. But even when things became extremely unpleasant and acrimonious, I would never, ever, say a bad word against Lesley. She was the best wife and the best mother that anyone could ever wish for. Things just went terribly wrong, and that was mainly my fault.

With hindsight, I now think that until Rita or any other woman came on the scene, there was a chance that Lesley would have possibly made me jump through hoops for a year or so longer and then we might have got back together.

But I didn't know that at the time. I thought that if she wanted a divorce, she wanted it to be over completely and that there was absolutely no chance for me. I honestly believed that I was officially divorced and she didn't want anything more to do with me. It wasn't until weeks later that I was told otherwise.

Of course, the horrendous publicity in the *Daily Mirror*, with days of being portrayed as some sort of vile maniac, the relationship that really suffered was between me and the children. Once Rita and I became public knowledge, I was no longer welcome at the house.

My solicitor tells me that I have every right to come and go as I please, but I can't do that without Lesley becoming hysterical and risking upsetting the children even further.

Once I tried to deliver some Easter eggs to re-establish a link with the children. But that went horribly wrong.

I went to Duffield hoping just to be able to speak to the children. I had a card and an Easter egg for each of them in a box and went round to the house. I did ring first to ask where I could leave them because I didn't want to go round to the house and cause trouble, but Lesley wasn't there so I thought I would just go and drop them off at the shop. I told the girl in the shop, and when I was walking towards it, Lesley came out and met me.

She walked towards me and we had this terrible row in the middle of the street. I gave her the box which held all the eggs and cards. She just kept saying, 'Take them back, I don't want them.'

She was screaming at me and I didn't know what to do. I didn't want to have a row so I just walked away. Lesley tore up all the letters I'd written to the children. I left. I just had to get out of there.

I was shocked and hurt. I went to my mum's in Alvaston. I was still shaking and we had a cup of tea and talked about what had happened. My mum wasn't very impressed with Lesley.

Then, later, Rita and I went to the Stanhope Lodge pub nearby for something to eat. As we were sitting there waiting for our food, Sophie stormed up to us and said, 'I want a word with you outside.'

'I'm not coming outside. I don't want to have a row with you.'

Then Sophie started screaming and insulted Rita, using absolutely foul language. In the end, the landlord asked her to leave the pub and told her not to come back. Her language was appalling.

I hope things with the children will be sorted out soon. There's an awful stalemate at the moment. It's all hideously new to me but I find the courts so antifathers. It's extraordinary — for five children and Lesley I was ordered to pay £500 per week. It seemed an enormous sum to me. Most people don't even earn that much.

I appealed against it because it is absurd, but you can't get blood out of a stone. I even laughed when I heard the order; I thought it was a joke. I earn £1,400 a week, which might sound a lot, but when you take out 12.5 per cent to my agent, tax and travelling, there is not much left. I want to care for my family and I always will, but the way this huge figure was imposed upon me was ghastly.

After Rita had had a painful series of operations on her feet, we stayed with Lionel Pickering and his family. For some reason, Lesley tried to ring me, but after so many shouting matches on the phone, I was not keen to talk to her.

Eventually, she tracked me down at Lionel's house. I still didn't want to speak but she tricked me by saying that one of the children was very ill. She knew that would bring me to the phone. Then she really shocked me again. She said, 'This is the last time I am asking you. You can come home. If you come now, I will come and get you, but this is your last chance. You have got to come now if you're going to come. Just say 'Yes' you want to come back home.'

I was terribly torn again, but I think I would have done just about anything to be with my children again. I said, 'Yes, that is what I want, I'll come back home.'

We arranged for a taxi to come and pick me up and I would go back home to my family and try to start again. I was so churned up inside I couldn't think straight. I would do anything for my children and I was missing them more than ever, so, even though I had no idea how Lesley and I could ever begin to pick up the pieces after what had happened between us, I was prepared to give it a try.

Of course, Rita was very upset. There we were, having a lovely family dinner at Lionel Pickering's house, and all of a sudden I was leaving them to go back to my wife.

But Rita is quite a lady. She has seen me suffer over not seeing the children. She said, 'If you want to see them, you have got to go back to Lesley. If that is what you want, I will ring you a taxi.' And she dialled for a taxi. Just as the cab was arriving, I rang Lesley back. She said 'Are you definitely coming?'

'Yes,' I said, 'The taxi is just arriving.'

Then Lesley said she had changed her mind. And she roared with cruel laughter down the telephone. I was absolutely shattered. Saying that she wanted me back and then telling me to get lost isn't exactly helping herself to get over it all and start a new life. I could never do things like that.

Of course, Rita and I had a few difficult moments but she understood. That is the wonderful thing about her; she understands.

Lesley has really stunned me with some of the things she has done. Before we split up, I was in hospital and I sent her some flowers, just to say 'I love you'. You don't just stop loving someone.

Then my father-in-law visited me with the children and came in with a bunch of flowers. I thought, 'That's nice, they've brought me some flowers,' but it was the same bunch that I had sent to Lesley. She was sending them back to me. I had included a card and written 'I love you' on it and she had replied by writing on the back, 'Give these to one of the bloody nurses.'

She can't be happy being endlessly bitter like this. Trying to trick someone just to hurt them is pathetic. She is desperate for Rita to know that I would prefer to be with her and the children. It must amaze and infuriate her to see that Rita has stood steadfastly by me throughout this.

Rita is extraordinary, so big-hearted and generous, she has helped me through everything. It has been like living through a horror film. It was actually worse than that, with everything manipulated for her desired effect.

I just hope I can come through all this and create some sort of relationship with my children. Poppy has been put in a terrible position. I suppose it is seen as disloyalty to her mother if she comes to see me. Lesley told me that Poppy, who is quite bright and, hopefully, heading for university, has seen her schoolwork show a big dip since all this trouble.

That upsets me. I don't know if Poppy got to see the letter I sent to her — I have only got Lesley's word for that. I wrote in the letter to Poppy how much Daddy wanted to come back and see them all. But I never got a reply.

My life is still in turmoil because I never know what Lesley is going to do next. In February this year, she suddenly staged a one-woman demonstration outside *The Bill* studios. She suddenly arrived carrying a placard saying I was failing in my duties as a loving father because I had missed out on some of the £500 payments.

Of course, she arrived with a journalist in tow and, naturally, she didn't tell the full story — about the money in our joint account; about the £12,000 in the building society that I gave her; or that her father is a very rich man and the very idea of her worrying about where the next mortgage payment is coming from is a joke. That would not have been nearly good enough copy for the *Daily Mail* which carried an exclusive report on Lesley's demonstration, possibly earning her more thousands of pounds.

She followed that up by going to Westminster and lobbying MPs about me as if I were some monstrous threat to national security. I don't mind for myself. Short of accusing me of starting World War II I don't think there is much left she can have a go at me for, but how does she think the children feel when they read this rubbish?

It is deplorable that a private matter should be dragged into the public domain. I thought it was desperately sad, and I'm afraid that she might have had some sort of breakdown. She stood outside the studios and, later, she even asked to be on Central TV. Of course I was upset, because I still have feelings for her. But it's absurd. She has plenty of money and the children, and I am left living in a little rented flat and owing the tax man a fortune.

The allegations about missing maintenance payments didn't really tell the whole story. They didn't take into account any of the joint money that Lesley took control of when I moved out. What she didn't reveal was that there is £4,500 in an account waiting to be unfrozen by the next court appearance for her. I just find that £500 a week is more than I can afford out of taxed income.

Lesley has got everything. I am living in a little flat with Rita, I have got a little bit in the building society but the reason I owe the tax man a fortune is that I have been wrongly advised in the past. But really I am just sad because of the kids. How do they feel when their mother's carrying on like that in public? They have to go to school the next day and face other kids. When I saw her with the placard and read all the articles I genuinely felt very sorry. She must be very unhappy.

But most of what she has said is simply not true. She called me a 'womaniser' which she knows is a lie. I never looked at another woman from the moment I met Lesley. I never even remotely wanted to, I was totally besotted with her. If I had been a womaniser, I would hardly have slogged home on the train to Duffield every night from my job in London.

Lesley says I was violent towards her, that I pinched her and even tore her clothes from her. It makes sensational tabloid newspaper reading, but that doesn't tell you exactly how it was.

Our rows were never as bad as she painted them. I loved her, I really did. Why else would I adopt her two children from her first marriage, have five of our own and then adopt a Romanian orphan baby? Lesley seems to want to try to rewrite our past, to blot out all the good times we had, in order to justify her hatred for me now. The worst thing of all is that she has turned the children against me.

It just seems so hard. Even if I'd been an absolute bastard to her and beaten her up and run off with an 18-year-old bimbo, I would be entitled to see my children.

Lesley is being very unreasonable. I am very sad that she has brought the children into this mess. Lesley says now, through her solicitors, that she is not actively influencing the children not to see me. She says that they can come and see me if they want to, but simply that they'd rather not.

It's hard to remain sane. The kids are my life. Not being able to see them is absolutely the worst agony. I don't know what information they are being fed, but they are clearly only hearing one side of the story. That's why I'm writing this book. I've written and I've telephoned but each time I've met with rebuttals so I am just trying to remain calm and not cause a scene. I just want to keep the peace, really. Lesley is still so bitter it's impossible for me to deal with her. But it's awful. I miss them so much. I can't put it into words how much I miss them.

Everything is stacked against fathers. Every available weapon is used. I am such an emotional person and I want to see the children so badly, I think about going to their school but I am terrified of causing an awful scene. Lesley has the ace up her sleeve because she knows that anything I do will go straight into the papers.

Lesley has said that she wouldn't mind if I ended up in one of those old actors' homes, having had a stroke and not being able to speak, with all these other old boys jabbering around me about famous parts that they had played. I thought, 'Crikey, she must hate me.' I keep coming back to 'Hell hath no fury like a woman scorned'. Perhaps it's the arrival of Rita on the scene that has upset her so much.

At work, with a script to learn and a busy schedule, I find I can just throw myself into work and forget about it all, but it's not easy. If I hear some of the other lads talking about their kids it can suddenly get to me. If I hadn't got somebody like Rita I would have gone under.

I can easily understand how people can feel so down

they end it all. I need another person, a rock to hang on to. Lesley was always exactly that for me. Now, lately, Rita has become that rock, and she has been wonderful. But it has taken its toll on me; my diabetes has been much worse and that is all down to stress.

I am not bitter. In a way, I still have feelings for Lesley, that is the really sad part. I know I can never live with her again but I know in my heart that I care for Lesley and love the children, I really do. I always will. I am sure that is why I dream about the children most nights. We were so complementary to each other, Lesley and I. It's just very sad that a relationship that was so good has turned out like this. I adore my kids and I miss them desperately.

Divorce was always something that happened to other people. I never thought that it could happen to me. What has happened to me seems strange and foreign and like something out of a horrific nightmare. I never imagined in my darkest moments that I would finish up like this.

I never considered a life without Lesley and the children and I certainly never wanted one. When they say there are no winners in a divorce, they are absolutely right. Everyone is a loser. I have lost my wife and family, and my family have lost me. The kids have lost a father, at least as a permanent presence. But they haven't lost me completely, not so long as I have breath left in my body.

I am very wary about the whole thing now. Lesley is like a loose cannon, someone who is not logical at the moment. She has told my driver in London that she will force me to my knees. I have every reason to be just as angry, but I would never say that.

When I was reduced to living back at my mother's, I

think Lesley was happy. It seems to me that Lesley expected me to carry on doing that for ever.

When I first met Lesley, and kissed her and touched her, I just knew that everything was right. It was love at first sight. I know now I am at least lucky to have had that. It was a great experience. We had a great passion for each other, both physically and emotionally. I suppose she can't bear that it doesn't exist any more. She has to blame someone, and that someone is me.

It is just not like her. She is not a cruel person, or I never thought she was. She was always an extremely kind-hearted and warm person. The way she has behaved is one of the cruellest things that has ever happened to me.

She has phoned Rita and had long chats with her. Rita says she starts off quite rationally, and then becomes angry. She was ringing Rita so much that she has had the phone number changed.

In my heart of hearts I know that, if we ever had got back together again, I think it would have been an impossible job. Too much has happened. But in the end it is not me that she wants. She doesn't want me back; the frightening thing is that she wants to destroy me.

I never thought it would ever get to this state, but, now it has, I want it to be as amicable as possible. I didn't think Lesley would use the children like this but people do strange things when emotions start flying about. I stayed at my mother's for six months living like a monk, but that wasn't enough.

I am so lucky to have found Rita. She is so cheerful and I think she has saved me. I was very low when I met her. I was very lonely and despairing, but I don't want to claim that I was on the verge of suicide. Even in my darkest moments, I have never seriously considered taking my own life as a way out. I don't think I could have gone through with it because I am frightened of dying.

Rita has been a great support, and has been totally understanding in all this. She is helping me most in trying to get back with the kids. That is what I want above everything else.

I learned through that article in the *Mail* that, even though James is dyslexic, there is a good chance he will be able to go to university. That makes me very proud, but I am so sad that I have to find out in an article that criticises me so bitterly, and not directly from Lesley or him.

I am still hoping to gain proper access. We went to court to start the wheels in motion but it is just such a long and painful process.

Lesley says that she is not actively encouraging the children to avoid contact with me. But, of course, she doesn't say what she has said to them about me. I was told by the child welfare officer to write to them all, which I did, and then I was to get a mobile phone, which I did, and give them all the number. I should then set aside a time between 6.00pm and 7.00pm on a Sunday night for the children to ring me.

I have done that for months since the last court hearing, and they haven't rung once. It is heart-breaking. The next step is through the child welfare officer who will hopefully set up a meeting between me and the three youngest. I don't know for certain that the kids are aware of the mobile phone.

My life now is very alien to me because I am such a family man. I go to football matches and see the players or supporters with their children and it brings an instant lump to my throat. It makes me very sad. I was very close to the children.

I haven't seen them for quite a while now. The arrival of Rita may have made them think that Daddy has not only left home but Daddy has also gone off with another woman. But that was never the case. It's a lot to cope with.

Thank God for *The Bill*. At dreadful times like this, I am glad I have got a demanding job that can take my mind off the personal pain that is rattling around in me. That has been my reaction — to bury myself in my work. It does help, but my feelings are still all very raw.

I am a long way from perfect but, in the great scheme of things, I don't think I did that much wrong. Some people don't work, gamble all their money away, chase after other women or beat their wives up. I never did any of those things. I just worked very, very hard and sometimes drank too much to help to keep myself going.

Lesley and I haven't talked for a bit because it has been too painful. At the moment, we are still both blaming each other for what went wrong.

I can't begin to understand what's going on in Lesley's mind. But she obviously has a problem about being the victim. She has turned it into some sort of campaign.

The last time we met face to face was in court. I brought a case to get access for the children, so we met then and it wasn't very pleasant. That was when the mobile phone idea was instituted. Lesley looked ill and that upset me, but she was still full of bitterness. She was with her sister who could barely talk to me. It was just a horrible experience.

You spend 22 years of your life with somebody and it ends up with you sitting at one end of a bench and her at the other, flanked by your solicitors. No talking to each other. Not even daring to look at each other. It's tragic.

It really hurt me and I just wanted to get out of that courtroom as soon as possible. I suppose if we hadn't cared so much about each other there wouldn't be this level of hatred now. Because hatred is passion. It's a very fine line between love and hate and if the marriage hadn't been so close, and it was bloody close, then we would both be happy to move on to the next stage of our lives.

Ian Peacock, my diabetic consultant, was with me while the divorce papers were being delivered to me in hospital and he said, 'I am sorry. I just can't believe this is happening. I don't know what to say. I have never seen anything like it in my life.' Even he tried to talk to Lesley and failed.

Our local doctor, Dr Barbara Leyland, went to see her. Friends also tried to see her, but nothing worked. Nothing would make her budge. She has always been a very determined lady, from the very first time I met her. If she set her mind on something there was nothing you could do to make her change. I'm sure she didn't believe that I would comply with all the conditions listed in the initial letter, but I did.

The letter suggested that she thought I was an alcoholic, but I have always known that I am not. I have always enjoyed a drink and I have always been inclined to drink too much.

I love pubs and the company, conversation and atmosphere that go along with them. I started drinking when I was young, but I've always been a social drinker. I loved Saturday night out on the town at the Locarno, a few pints and then chatting up the women. It's amazing how three or four pints loosen your tongue and makes conversation easier. Five or six pints made it a lot harder.

But I am not an alcoholic. I just like a drink. I don't get angry or violent when I'm drunk, I just get slower and slower and eventually I go to sleep and then the next day I don't fancy a drink.

Lesley has got a thing about drink and the fear of what drink can do to people has always been firmly imprinted on her mind. Even though I met her in a wine bar, she never liked visiting pubs. I believe Lesley found it hard to accept that I felt differently. Certainly, there have been occasions, and plenty of them, when I have got drunk. But I happily enjoy weeks without alcohol. I love the chat, and every now and then, I like to have a few too many. I don't need the stuff. I just drink when I want to.

All the publicity has been very hurtful and designed to cause maximum upset to Rita and I. *Mirror* reporter Rod Chaytor spoke to Rita near our home and wanted her side of the story. He has tried three times to offer her money, and he has tried to collar me. But the *Mirror* is in constant touch about everything I do. I can't breathe without people telling Lesley and then it ending up in the newspapers. Rita has suffered badly. She can hardly mention Lesley's name.

Rita says now that when we first met, I was just about as low as anyone can go. I was desperate. It's always very sad when a marriage breaks down but when a good marriage collapses in the full glare of publicity, it is very hard to bear.

Rita rescued me then. She saved me from going under, giving me her unconditional love. That gave me a reason for living. She showed me how foolish I was for allowing another person to affect me so badly. I don't think I could have recovered on my own. Rita helped me wake up and gave me the strength to battle back.

At my lowest moments, I used to sit sobbing on my own. I am not ashamed to say that, for a while, I used to cry myself to sleep night after night. Often, sleep would not come, and I would lie there sobbing like a baby. My dear mum was so good to me and I will always be grateful to her.

But I couldn't see a way out of the hole until Rita came along. The things that had always meant everything to me in my life — Lesley and the kids — had been taken away. It was a desperately sorry state to be in. Nothing seemed to matter.

Then Rita came to the rescue, and has helped me to feel energetic and ambitious for the future. I am now very career-minded again, when I once felt so depressed and apathetic. And to think that it was just a chance meeting at a football match which brought me this wonderful woman — Rita's incredible, selfless love has changed my life again.

It was my birthday on 28th March 1997. I was 48. I didn't get a card from any of the children. I didn't get a card from Lesley either, though I hardly expected one. And I didn't even get a card from my mother as we weren't getting on too well at the time.

I received just four cards and they were all from Rita and her family. Rita was angry on my behalf and she was going to ring Lesley and tell her how disgraceful she thought it was. Rita thought Lesley could at least have got the children to send me a card, but in the end, she couldn't bring herself to talk to her. It is very hard when you wake up on your birthday and not one of your children are inclined to send you a card. It would have meant so much.

My greatest fear is that the longer it goes on, the harder it becomes for the children to meet me, and the more awkward it will be when we do meet up again. Above all else, I am absolutely determined one day to have a relationship again with my children. But the gap is gradually becoming harder and harder to bridge.

I think about them every day. Often, late at night, I just burst into tears thinking about the children and wondering what they are doing. I heard second- or third-hand that Poppy has won a hockey trophy or that James is going to university, and I am terribly proud and upset that I haven't been able to hear about it from them.

My only hope is that, one day, the children will make up their own minds about what has happened and I will be able to see them again.

This book is my way of explaining my side of the whole story. I have been an actor now for 24 years. Apart from a three-month period very early on, I have never been out of work which is quite remarkable in my business. I have worked my socks off for my family. I always dreamed about us having a nice, big family house in the country. And I was chuffed to bits when I was able to buy us one.

Perhaps I worked too hard. Michael Chapman, the boss at *The Bill*, has been very supportive. He went berserk when Lesley was outside doing her one-woman protest. They don't like any sort of negative publicity and I don't blame them. Neither do I.

Financially, Lesley has done extremely well. There are not many actors' wives who are set up like she is. But I suppose it is so bitter and acrimonious now because we cared about each other so deeply. If we had had no feelings about each other there wouldn't be all this animosity.

I would go and see the kids like thousands of other disappointed divorced dads and we would all get on with our lives. I'd just pick them up, say 'Hi' and that would be that. It was never like that with us. There is a wall of animosity between us now and I don't know how to get through it.

I don't believe it is in anyone's interest for the children not to have a good relationship with me. I have just got to bide my time until they are ready. Friends have suggested that I call at the school and try to talk to them on their own. I am sorely tempted to do it, but I don't want to cause a scene at the school that would finish up in all the papers.

More importantly I just don't think it would be the right thing to do. I desperately don't want to embarrass them in front of their friends.

Rita has had to take me on with all this emotional baggage, and she's been great. It is her and my job that is keeping me sane.

I am not one to cry on people's shoulders, but I have been hurt very badly by what has happened to me in the past year or so. I am a very independent bloke and although I am lucky enough to have quite a few people I regard as close friends, I have never really wanted to burden anyone with my problems. It's also embarrassing because most people, like Victoria Wood, for example, whom I'm very friendly with, are also good friends of Lesley's as well. June Brown has been wonderful, but she's a family friend.

The last thing in the world I'd want is to force our friends to take sides. I don't think that's right. That's why I don't like Lesley bringing everything out into the public arena, because it's got nothing to do with anybody but us really. It should be a private and personal thing. Whatever we are going through, however difficult, should be just between us.

Lesley's protest outside *The Bill* studios absolutely astonished me. She actually said that if I lost my job over it, she'd be glad. It's crazy. If I lost my job I wouldn't have any money, and neither would Lesley. What sort of thinking is that?

I don't think this is anything to do with money. I think her protest with her placard outside the studios was simply designed to embarrass me. To show me how she feels.

Rita can't have any more children. She has had a hysterectomy. But, in any case, I am very happy with the children I've got. I am very proud of them and I still dream about them every night. The most difficult thing about all this is not seeing them.

When *The Bill* won the National Television Award for best drama serial in the summer of 1996, I put my wedding ring back on before the announcement, just for luck and also because I thought that if we did win it, most of my life and most of my reasons for winning it were due to Lesley and the kids.

Lesley is an amazing woman, a genuine mistress of all trades. She is a brilliant cook. She was, without doubt, the most brilliant mother and a marvellous wife. I can't close the door on that part of my life. It meant a great deal to me to think that Lesley and the family had helped me to win that award. I wanted Lesley and the children to be part of my success. They deserve it. It's taken me more than 20 years to get to this point and a lot of my success is down to them.

They say that behind every successful man is a great woman, and that was certainly true of me; I could never have done it without her. I put the ring on because I wanted her to be with me in some way.

It was great to win, and a big surprise. I didn't know it was going to be the Duchess of York giving us the award. I was delighted to meet her, and when she walked down the stairs I thought, 'Crikey!' It was a great honour and a great treat.

I just kissed her on the spur of the moment, but she seemed to be quite receptive. You don't usually get the chance to meet people like that, but she just whispered in my ear how much she really liked the programme, that she was a great fan, that she thought we deserved to win the award and how much she liked my character. A quick kiss and away.

I was thinking this morning about the best family times. I go over and over in my mind how Poppy came and cuddled me in bed in the morning. Moments like that are my happiest memories and I miss them so much.

The four of them, James, Henry, Poppy and Edward used to pop into bed with me and have pillow fights. They would hold me down and give me 30 seconds to escape. They were wonderful, wonderful times and the tragedy is that you don't realise at the time just how wonderful they are.

I don't think Lesley has ever been involved with anyone else. I'm sure that if she was, it would bother me every bit as much as Rita has bothered her. That is the one thing I am dreading. I haven't heard anything for a while but I am expecting, sooner or later, another bloke to appear on the scene and I am honest enough to admit that that will devastate me, even though I'm not at home or part of her life in any meaningful way at the moment.

If my marriage is over then that is awful, but fair enough. I still want to have a relationship with my children and with their children. No one has the right to take that away from me. In some ways, maybe I have played it too fair, but I didn't know any other way of behaving. It is the worst thing that can happen. I told my friends at *The Bill*, 'Don't ever get in this position whereby your marriage goes like this, it's just horrendous.'

My colleagues at *The Bill* have been very supportive. I find it very difficult to talk about the whole thing, and you don't want people saying how sorry they are all the time. So, unless I'm asked, I don't talk about it at all. They have met Lesley and they are totally baffled at the way she is behaving.

When I began writing this book, after the painful details of our split had been turned into breakfast entertainment in the morning papers, I really believed that however acrimonious it became, somehow Lesley and I would get back together, if only for the children's sake.

Now I know that that is not going to happen. Events have just snowballed out of my control. Now Lesley is too angry, too bitter, and we both have to start to carve out separate lives. Unfortunately, it has gone way past the point of no return. I've accepted that now, and I have learned to be realistic. I don't want it to affect the children any more, and simply want them to have the opportunity to hear my side of the story.

I know it will be different with Rita but I know that we will be very happy together. We won't have any children, I realise that, although I think we would if we could. I would never stop.

It is more than 18 months since I last saw the children and my deepest fear is that a dreadful, unbridgeable gulf will come between us.

Children see things in black and white. Unfortunately, life simply isn't like that. They know Mummy is on her own feeling sad and lonely. What they don't know is that Daddy feels sad and lonely, too. But unlike their mother, I have no Mark, no Sophie, no James, no Poppy, no Henry, no Edward and no Elly. It feels as though someone has pulled out the plug on my life-support machine but the pain goes on.

I am still suffering, still feeling this terrible void that ahunts me every minute of the day. Being denied the right to see my children is literally breaking my heart.

Of course, they feel tremendous loyalty to their mum because their dad has left them all for another woman. That is not true at all. It simply did not happen like that. But that is how they must see it and I completely understand. They think Daddy is living with another woman and Daddy is happy with her. The younger ones are not old enough to understand anything else, and the older ones are acting out of support for their mum, which is perfectly natural.

One of my main goals is to avoid upsetting the children as much as possible. But by doing that, I have probably encouraged them to feel that I have neglected them. I don't feel that I have — they are hardly ever out of my thoughts.

I wake up thinking of happier times when we had

wonderful family holidays and outings and I replay favourite family moments over and over again. My instinct was to meet them from school and call and see as much of them as possible, but I felt right from the start that the more involved they became in the difficulties between Lesley and me, then the more I would upset them.

I have never sold my side of the story to the newspapers, insulted Lesley in the way she laid into me, and I never will. The main reason is that I do not want to hurt them.

This book is for my children. I want them to read it and understand my side of the sad break-up. I want them to know that I love them and I think about them all the time. I want them to know that I am so deeply sorry that I have hurt them by hurting their mother. And I want them to know, that even if they never see me or speak to me again, I will never stop loving them. This book is for my children and it is Daddy's way of putting his side across and saying 'sorry'.

Men don't seem to come out of a marriage split very well. For an actor who started off with nothing I had not done badly until the break-up. I have brought up seven children and provided a lovely family house for them. But now, after 24 years of hard work, I have ended up with nothing. I am more broke now than I was when I started.

Yet it is not the money I am bothered about. The deepest hurt is the children — I desperately want to see the kids. The hurt between me and Lesley is still so deep at the moment. It is not hatred, it is hurt. I think she is hurting just as much as I am. It's a horrible feeling.

It is absolutely dreadful to have to talk to a stranger

about whether or not you can see your own children. You feel you just shouldn't have to have the conversations. Recently, the child welfare officer told me that, at the moment, she felt the younger children would be upset at seeing me, and the older ones felt they did not want to see me at present. It was a real body-blow to hear that. They have never heard my side of the story. All they know is that Daddy is living with another woman and they are supporting their mum.

Sometimes, I pinch myself to make sure I'm not dreaming. My whole life has been taken away from me in a way I did not think would be possible. It's like some awful play or film with not the remotest prospect of a happy ending.

I am not bitter. I still think the world of Lesley, whatever she has said about me. I can't change that. Everybody says I should not feel like that, they say I should draw a line and move on, but it is not as easy as that. I can almost understand the things that she has done. She is so hurt that she lashes out. She is doing everything she can do to get her own back at me.

Whenever I get a quiet moment I think about the children. I try not to get depressed, just to think of the happy times.

Elly is beautiful now, which is so strange because, when we adopted her, she was a very odd-looking little bundle. It sounds awful, but I mean it with affection when I say she was the ugliest little baby you've ever seen.

Now she is so pretty and the weirdest thing is that she has developed into a real Lloyd. When the family went out together she looked like one of us. She is gorgeous and I know that she desperately wants to see me. She wants to see Daddy and she can't understand why that is forbidden. 'Where has Daddy gone to?' she asks. 'Is he away working?' She said to the welfare officer, 'I love my Daddy. If only he drank Coca-Cola we would be all right.'

The welfare officer thinks she is too young to see me now. She is just a gorgeous little girl who is full of life. She is very bright. People say she is lucky to have been adopted by us because she has turned out so perfectly, but I think we are lucky to have her. She is wonderful, adored by everyone.

Then there is Edward who is seven. I adore him like all the others, but he is frailer than them. He is very sensitive. Edward and I were very close, but he is very much his mother's boy. He is not struggling at school but it's not easy for him.

I think the two youngest ones are missing me the most, because it is hardest for them to understand why things can't be the same as they were. When he was asked about me he just started crying. And, of course, he was at the centre of the incident with the in-laws when I lost my temper over not being allowed to take him to the football match. I'm afraid it upset him more than any of the others, because he was there and he heard the row.

Henry is the joker of the family. He wants to see me very much but my kids stick together and, at the moment, I think he would feel disloyal to the others if he tried to see me on his own. Things are very black and white to Henry.

He probably can't understand what Daddy is doing living with another woman and why Daddy used to shout, have rows with Mummy and go out, instead of staying in and watching telly with him. He never understood why I used to have to work so much. Because of his nature, he can probably cope with what has happened better than the others, but I know it must hurt him very much. He is a very caring boy.

Poppy is the one I worry about more than any of the others, not because I love her any more but because there was a special bond between us. I miss that very much. We were very close and I hope we still are. I found it incredibly hurtful that I had caused such unhappiness for my daughter.

She was certainly heading for a university place before all this happened, and if she is not doing so well now then I know my behaviour has been a factor. She is very good at sport and very sensitive, and maybe the most caring of all my children. I know this break-up will probably affect her for ever and that causes me a lot of grief in my darker moments. Unless things can be sorted out amicably, she will not see her dad.

James is dyslexic but, funnily enough, he has developed into a very tough young man at the age of 18. He is very supportive of his mum. We used to have great fun together.

We had James just after we had lost Chloe. We probably pampered him far too much. He screamed for the first three months and we never had a decent night's sleep but we never minded because we wanted him so much.

He has really developed and there is a very good chance that he will go to university. He is very protective of Lesley in a very nice way which I admire greatly. I wouldn't want him any other way, even though everything I do is wrong and he is protecting his mum. James has taken over the mantle of leader of the house and I think he is coping with it really well.

He is the most critical of me at the moment, but I am very, very proud of him.

I have tried desperately to understand what is going on inside Lesley's mind. I am completely baffled by her now. The woman I see across the courtroom seems a totally different person to the woman I happily lived with for 20 years. I honestly don't think I have changed.

Sometimes, I just feel that my whole life has been taken away from me. Everyone has rows, but they never imagine that their life is going to be whipped away from under them without being able to do a thing about it.

One day I was married to a wife I loved with a huge and happy family and a lovely country house, and the next, the whole thing has gone and your wife is telling the world what a monster she has been living with. It's very difficult.

Now my main aim is to re-establish some sort of a relationship with the children. I am very wary of doing anything because I don't want to do anything that will hurt them in any way. They have been through so much in the last year or so, the last thing we need are any more rows. It must have been horrible for them at school so I am treading very carefully.

Everybody tells me that it will take time and, as the kids grow up, they will come back to me. I hope that's true. I still write to them and send cards and presents, but I don't get anything back. I assume they receive them. I don't know how much pressure is being put on them. Perhaps they just feel that replying would be disloyal to their mum.

Rita has been wonderful throughout all this. She has

had a tremendous amount to put up with. I don't know how she has done it. She must have wondered what she was taking on when she suddenly found the Press chasing after her and trying to get her story. She has refused all that and she has stood by me through thick and thin, and I can't praise her too highly.

My mum told me the other day that I am incredibly lucky to have met her. She has given me magnificent support at a time when I most needed it. I couldn't have faced all this criticism without having someone like her to hold my hand and love me in the way she has.

She has been amazingly selfless because she has loved me unconditionally. She has done it without ever wanting anything back. It can't have been easy for her. Her private life suddenly became front page news. That takes some coping with. She is photographed everywhere she goes and has to be careful about everything she says. She has never lived in that world.

I have been an actor for years and working in popular television shows brings you into the public eye, but even I have not been prepared for the level of interest. So how on earth Rita, who never wanted to be famous, has coped so brilliantly, I don't think I'll ever know.

When the news first broke and the journalists arrived at her flat, she was absolutely terrified. Two big blokes were outside ringing the bell. They wore smart suits so she thought they were the police, but when she opened the door, one of them put his foot against it and the other started taking photographs. She had no idea what was happening. At first, they wouldn't even tell her who they were. She's lovely to have taken all that in her stride.

Her parents, Ron and Beattie, must have been baffled too. The *Mirror* is her dad's paper, and to see their daughter's new bloke suddenly plastered all over it must have made them wonder what on earth she was getting mixed up in. They have been great, great people.

I do feel I have come through an awful lot since Lesley and I first fell out. I still think it is just crazy that Lesley and I have both thrown away so much. I don't think either of us wanted to part. But I have to steel myself to move on.

It might sound corny to count your blessings, but why not? I have been very, very lucky with women in my life. Hilary was a great love when I was a young man. Lesley was a fantastic wife and mother to my children.

And now Rita is a wonderful love who has helped me to come through the most difficult time in my life. I have been a very lucky man. When I was younger, I went out with lots of lovely girls, but I have had those three tremendous women who have shared my life. Maybe that is why I am not bitter about what has happened. Of course, there has been terrible heart-break and I am still upset about not seeing my children, but I believe that will eventually turn out all right with time.

Some men go through their whole lives without ever falling in love. It has happened to me three times. That has got to be lucky, hasn't it?